Depression Book For Men

Crafted by Skriuwer

Copyright © 2024 by Skriuwer.

All rights reserved. No part of this book may be used or reproduced in any form whatsoever without written permission except in the case of brief quotations in critical articles or reviews.

For more information, contact : **kontakt@skriuwer.com** (www.skriuwer.com)

TABLE OF CONTENTS

CHAPTER 1: UNDERSTANDING DEPRESSION IN MEN

- Explains why depression in men can look different from women.
- Shows how social pressures and self-stigma delay help.
- Stresses the importance of recognizing early signs and seeking support.

CHAPTER 2: COMMON CAUSES OF DEPRESSION

- Identifies key factors like life changes, stress, and unresolved trauma.
- Covers biological and environmental triggers that raise the risk.
- Emphasizes the need to spot these causes early for better outcomes.

CHAPTER 3: WARNING SIGNS AND SYMPTOMS

- Discusses physical and emotional clues of hidden sadness.
- Highlights how men often show irritability or anger instead of tears.
- Explains how spotting these signs can prevent deeper struggles.

CHAPTER 4: WHY MEN HIDE THEIR FEELINGS

- Reveals cultural and personal beliefs that push men to stay silent.
- Describes how denial and embarrassment worsen sadness.
- Offers tips to move past the "tough guy" image and open up safely.

CHAPTER 5: BREAKING HARMFUL HABITS

- Shows how small unhealthy routines fuel negative moods.
- Gives methods to replace or reduce bad habits step by step.
- Encourages forming boundaries and support for long-term change.

CHAPTER 6: HELPFUL TOOLS FOR THE MIND

- Presents practical techniques like breathing drills and journaling.
- Explains how mindfulness and physical exercise boost emotional health.
- Urges consistent practice to strengthen coping and resilience.

CHAPTER 7: HOW TO REACH OUT FOR HELP

- *Guides men on where to turn—friends, family, professionals.*
- *Discusses common barriers, such as fear of judgment.*
- *Reminds readers that seeking support is an act of strength, not weakness.*

CHAPTER 8: PHYSICAL HEALTH AND THE MIND

- *Links nutrition, exercise, and hormones to mood stability.*
- *Shows how better sleep and stress control impact mental well-being.*
- *Suggests small, consistent changes to form healthier habits.*

CHAPTER 9: WORK, STRESS, AND FEELING LOW

- *Examines job pressures that lead to burnout or sadness.*
- *Offers tips for setting boundaries, time management, and self-care at work.*
- *Encourages healthy conversations with bosses and coworkers about stress.*

CHAPTER 10: FAMILY AND RELATIONSHIP PRESSURES

- *Explores conflicts at home, from parenting strains to marital tension.*
- *Shows how communication and boundary-setting can reduce domestic stress.*
- *Highlights teamwork and open talks to preserve supportive relationships.*

CHAPTER 11: CHANGING NEGATIVE THOUGHT PATTERNS

- *Details common thinking errors that fuel sadness.*
- *Provides steps for challenging harmful beliefs with realistic ones.*
- *Explains how to reduce self-criticism and nurture a kinder internal voice.*

CHAPTER 12: PRACTICAL DAILY EXERCISES

- *Suggests quick, doable actions to maintain emotional balance.*
- *Includes routines like mindfulness, short workouts, and gratitude practice.*
- *Shows how to adapt these exercises to fit a busy lifestyle.*

CHAPTER 13: BUILDING STRONG FRIENDSHIPS

- *Explains why men benefit greatly from supportive peer bonds.*
- *Offers ways to find new friends or deepen current connections.*
- *Covers conflict resolution, trust, and keeping friendships strong over time.*

CHAPTER 14: SETTING GOALS FOR IMPROVEMENT

- *Explains the SMART method and how to track steady progress.*
- *Advises on handling slips in motivation or over-ambition.*
- *Shows how achieving small targets builds confidence and resilience.*

CHAPTER 15: MEDICATION AND OTHER TREATMENTS

- *Covers different antidepressants, their uses, and potential side effects.*
- *Introduces therapies like TMS or ECT for severe cases.*
- *Stresses the value of combining medication with therapy and self-care.*

CHAPTER 16: HANDLING SETBACKS

- *Normalizes temporary relapses and highlights early warning signs.*
- *Shows how to prevent a short dip from becoming a deep crisis.*
- *Emphasizes self-compassion and adjusting routines when things go wrong.*

CHAPTER 17: STAYING MOTIVATED FOR CHANGE

- *Examines why energy fades and how to reignite it.*
- *Describes using accountability, rewards, and social support.*
- *Reveals how to push past plateaus without burning out.*

CHAPTER 18: SHARING YOUR STORY

- *Discusses personal benefits and social impact of talking about sadness.*
- *Gives tips on choosing the right audience and level of detail.*
- *Explores how openness can reduce stigma and help others feel less alone.*

CHAPTER 19: RESOURCES FOR ONGOING SUPPORT

- *Lists local groups, hotlines, and online services men can tap into.*
- *Mentions financial aid, specialized clinics, and faith-based supports.*
- *Encourages using these resources to stay stable and avoid deeper lows.*

CHAPTER 20: PLANNING FOR A BETTER FUTURE

- *Shows how to form a personal wellness blueprint for long-term growth.*
- *Warns against overconfidence and outlines crisis backup plans.*
- *Explores adding new skills, balanced routines, and deeper life purposes.*

CHAPTER 1: UNDERSTANDING DEPRESSION IN MEN

Depression is a serious condition that causes long-lasting sadness, loss of interest in daily activities, and sometimes feelings of worthlessness. When a man is depressed, he might hide his emotions behind anger, isolation, or unusual actions. Many men do not like to talk about feeling down, so they may pretend that they are fine. This can lead to more serious problems over time.

In this chapter, we will talk about how depression can affect men in ways that might differ from women. We will also look at why many men keep their sadness to themselves. By understanding how this condition appears, we can learn ways to tackle it early. Please note that sadness is not a weakness. It is a health problem that can be handled with clear steps and the right support.

---

1. The Basic Idea of Depression

Depression is not the same as feeling sad for a short while. It lasts for weeks, months, or even years if a person does not get help. It can show itself through changes in mood, thinking, and behavior. Some people might lose interest in the things that once made them happy. Others might feel tired or have trouble sleeping. Depression is not a problem of being "lazy" or "unwilling to try." It is a true health condition that affects the way a person's brain works.

When we talk about men and depression, there can be more hidden signs. Some men do not show the typical sadness or crying that people often connect with depression. Instead, they might become more irritable or want to spend a lot of time alone. This difference in behavior can make it harder for other people to see that something is wrong. As a result, many men do not receive help until their depression is quite severe.

It helps to keep in mind that no two people have the exact same reaction to depression. It can appear at different ages, in different forms, and with different intensities. Some men might feel depressed only once in their life, while others might have repeated episodes of low mood. Knowing these facts helps us avoid making assumptions or blaming ourselves or others. Depression is not a choice. It is a complex mix of internal and external factors that can be managed if found early.

2. How Depression Looks Different in Men

Men are raised in many cultures to be tough, strong, and in control. They might have grown up hearing messages like "boys don't cry" or "man up." These ideas can shape how a man deals with sadness. Instead of talking about feeling low, a man may feel forced to keep it inside. Over time, holding in sadness can turn into anger, reckless behavior, or aggression.

Here are some ways depression might appear in men:

- **Anger or frustration:** Some men might find themselves snapping at loved ones over small issues. They might feel a constant sense of annoyance with the world around them.
- **Risky behaviors:** A depressed man might start gambling, driving too fast, or drinking more alcohol. He might do these things without thinking about the dangers to himself or others. This type of behavior can be a way to mask deep sadness.
- **Staying silent:** A man might throw himself into his job or other activities to avoid facing his low moods. He could spend long hours at work, avoiding family and friends. This can cause more stress and pressure.
- **Unusual bodily aches:** Depression is not just a mental concern; it can also cause headaches, digestive issues, or back pain. Some men might visit a doctor for these physical complaints but never mention they have been feeling down.
- **Sudden changes in eating or sleeping:** A man might eat much more or much less than normal. He might also sleep too much or struggle to fall asleep and stay asleep.

These signs can build upon each other. When sadness continues for a long time, it can affect many areas of life, from personal relationships to job performance. By recognizing that these behaviors might be clues of depression, men can take the first step to get help.

---

3. The Role of Stigma

Stigma is a set of negative beliefs and attitudes about something that many people do not understand well. When it comes to mental health, stigma can stop men from speaking up. They may worry that others will see them as weak. They might also fear that admitting to depression could affect their career or personal reputation. This fear leads to more silence, which can make the depression much worse.

It helps to know that the human brain and body can get sick just like any other part of us. There is no shame in having an emotional problem. In fact, many big companies and social organizations now realize that mental health is as important as physical health. When men push past the stigma, they give themselves a chance to learn more about their struggles. This often brings relief because they can see that they are not alone in their situation.

Another major factor is how family and friends might react. Some men worry that talking about low mood could make their loved ones see them differently. Yet, many people respond with understanding. Once they learn that depression is a real condition and not a personal failing, they can give support. This can be a key turning point in recovery. Instead of facing sadness alone, a man might have someone to talk to. That sense of connection often reduces shame and encourages action.

---

4. Differences in Brain Chemistry and Hormones

Depression involves changes in brain chemicals known as neurotransmitters. These are natural substances that help send messages through the brain and the rest of the body. When levels of certain chemicals (such as serotonin or norepinephrine) are off-balance, it can lead to low mood, anxiety, and other issues. Men and women share these basic processes, but there can be differences in how hormones interact with these chemicals.

For example, testosterone levels can play a role in how men handle stress and sadness. Low testosterone might make a man feel more tired, more sad, and less interested in activities. On the other hand, a spike in stress hormones like cortisol can also add to the risk of depression. Hormones do not tell the whole story, but they are part of the larger picture that includes genetics, personal history, and life environment.

Learning about these details helps remove blame and shame. Depression is not just about willpower or trying harder. Biological factors matter, and it is wise to keep that in mind when choosing support or treatment. This also means that some forms of help might work better for certain men, depending on how their hormones and brain chemicals behave. A man might see a doctor and find that hormone treatment, or a change in diet, might help ease some symptoms.

5. How Environment and Upbringing Can Add Pressure

A man's environment includes his home, his workplace, and his social circles. All of these can have a direct or indirect effect on his mental state. If a man grows up in a house where there is constant conflict or strict rules about showing emotion, he might learn to hide his feelings. If his work environment is stressful or lacks support, he might face high pressure daily. Over time, this ongoing stress can contribute to depression.

Another factor is how a man's parents or caregivers talked about sadness. If they never discussed sadness at home, or if tears were punished, it can shape how he sees mental health. He might believe that admitting to low mood is wrong. This learned attitude can stick with a person into adulthood, making it very hard for him to talk about how he feels.

In some families, men may be expected to provide financially no matter what. This can set a high bar for success. If a man loses his job or struggles at work, he might feel a deep sense of shame. He might think he failed as a provider. These negative thoughts can spiral into depression if not handled early. Another angle to consider is peer pressure from friends. Some groups might tease or mock any sign of sadness, calling it "soft." This only adds to the reluctance many men have about speaking up.

---

6. Why Men Often Wait Too Long to Get Help

Many men do not seek help until their symptoms are severe. There are many reasons for this. One is the fear of seeming incapable or less manly in front of others. Another reason is the idea that a "real man" should handle problems on his own. Men might also think their feelings are not serious enough to require expert help. As the sadness deepens, some men might become numb to their own emotions and think it is normal to feel empty.

There can also be a lack of knowledge about how to seek help. A man might not know where to start. Does he talk to a close friend, or should he go straight to a mental health professional? If he has never seen a counselor before, it might feel strange or uncomfortable to book that first appointment. Money can be another barrier, as therapy sessions and certain treatments can be expensive if not covered by insurance or workplace benefits.

Delaying help can lead to serious outcomes, including lost jobs, broken relationships, or self-harm. Addressing the problem early can save a lot of pain. It might feel scary at first, but many men later say that the relief of having someone understand is far greater than any fear they had. The earlier a man takes steps to handle depression, the sooner he can start feeling better.

---

7. Key Facts and Less-Known Details

There are some pieces of information about men's depression that are not always highlighted in common discussions. These details can be useful for those who want a better understanding:

1. **Depression can show itself in physical ways:** Men might visit the doctor more often for back pain, headaches, or stomach issues. It might take time for someone to connect these physical complaints to an underlying mood problem.
2. **High-functioning depression is common among men:** Some men continue to go to work, pay bills, and handle day-to-day tasks even when they feel hopeless. This high-functioning form of depression can go unnoticed for a long time.
3. **Men might use anger to hide deeper pain:** Instead of showing sadness, men can appear aggressive. This anger might be turned inward as well, leading to thoughts of self-blame.
4. **Certain groups of men face higher risks:** Men who experience big changes in life, such as divorce, retirement, or job loss, might be more at risk. Soldiers returning from military service are also at a higher risk due to traumatic experiences.
5. **Weak support networks:** Men often have fewer close friendships compared to women. This can mean they have fewer people to talk to when they are feeling low.

These facts highlight that depression in men is not always obvious. It can sit below the surface, only showing up in unexpected ways. This is why experts recommend that men try to be aware of their mood changes and reach out if they notice a shift in how they feel.

---

8. The Importance of Self-Awareness

Self-awareness means paying attention to how you feel physically and mentally. It also means noticing any changes in your behavior. For example, if you find that you are getting mad easily or feel tired all the time, that might be a sign of a deeper issue. Men who practice self-awareness are better able to spot red flags in their mood or daily habits.

One method to build self-awareness is to keep track of small details in your life. Some people use a simple notebook to write down their sleep patterns, eating habits, and mood each day. Others might use a phone app for this purpose. After a few weeks, you might see patterns, such as feeling more stressed after a lack of sleep or noticing that certain events trigger sad feelings. Once you spot these patterns, you can plan ways to handle them. This does not fix everything at once, but it does help you stay connected with your own state of mind.

Recognizing that you need help is not giving up. It is a sign of a responsible person who wants to do better. Men who learn to be open with themselves about their struggles are often the ones who succeed in getting the right help. They stop viewing depression as something that will go away on its own. Instead, they treat it as a real concern that deserves care and attention.

---

9. The Problem with Denial

Denial is a mental process where a person refuses to accept or acknowledge an uncomfortable truth. In the case of depression, a man might tell himself that he is just stressed or tired. He might ignore the fact that his mood is constantly low. This denial can delay help for months or years. It can also lead to an increase in harmful coping methods, like substance use.

When a man is in denial, he might come up with excuses for why he feels the way he does. He could blame his boss, his partner, or the weather. While external factors do play a role in how we feel, denial blocks the process of looking deeper. This can create a cycle where problems keep piling up. Eventually, something breaks, such as losing a job or a close relationship. By then, the depression can be quite severe.

The good news is that a person can break out of denial by being honest with himself and with others. This might begin with reading a book like this one or having a long talk with a trusted friend. Once a man admits he might have depression, he has taken the biggest step toward getting better. The rest of the steps might be uncomfortable, but they will lead to better health in the long term.

10. Building a Foundation of Knowledge

Understanding how depression works is like learning the rules of a sport. The more you know about it, the more prepared you are to handle it. For many men, knowledge about depression can remove the shame they feel. They see it as a medical condition rather than a sign of personal failure.

Learning the facts can also help you recognize if you or someone you know might be at risk. You can share this knowledge with family members, coworkers, or friends. They might not realize that men can experience different signs of depression. By explaining this, you can start open conversations that reduce stigma.

Another important reason to learn more about depression is to become a smarter consumer of mental health services. Not all treatments are the same. Some might be more effective for certain types of people. The ability to ask the right questions can help you find a therapist or doctor who truly understands your needs. With a strong foundation of knowledge, you can be an active participant in your own care.

11. Putting This Chapter into Practice

- **Try to list your personal signs of low mood:** Think back over the last few months. Have you noticed any changes in the way you sleep, eat, or spend your free time? Do you feel more irritable than normal? Write these observations down.
- **Talk to at least one trusted person:** Share some of your worries. You do not have to open up fully right away, but even a small step can help. See how it feels to say, "I've been feeling off for a while."
- **Observe other men around you:** You might see signs of hidden sadness. Sometimes noticing it in others can help you spot it in yourself. This does not mean you should diagnose them. Just become more aware of how men might act when they are down.

By doing these small tasks, you can begin to build awareness. This is often the first step toward addressing depression effectively.

12. Chapter Summary

Depression in men can look different than it does in women. It is often hidden behind anger or a constant need to stay busy. Social expectations and personal fears can make it hard for men to admit they are feeling low. Yet, understanding depression and recognizing its signs can help break down these barriers.

Knowledge is power. By learning about the biological and social factors of depression, men can see that it is not their fault. They can also see that help is available. Self-awareness is a key skill, allowing men to track changes in mood and take action early. Denial only makes things worse in the long run. Facing the truth can be a relief, because it opens the door to solutions.

This chapter covered the basics of how depression affects men. In the next chapter, we will look at the common causes of depression, including stressful life events and deeper underlying issues. By learning about the different factors that can lead to depression, men will have a clearer picture of what might trigger or worsen their low mood.

Remember, reaching out for help is not a sign of weakness. It takes courage to acknowledge the facts about how you feel. If you sense that you or someone close to you might be depressed, keep an open mind about the possibility of getting professional help. Early steps can make a big difference.

CHAPTER 2: COMMON CAUSES OF DEPRESSION

Depression in men can arise due to many reasons. Sometimes, it is one big event, like losing a job or going through a separation. Other times, it can be a series of smaller setbacks that build up over time. Understanding the root causes of depression helps men see why they feel the way they do. This chapter will focus on different common causes, from external triggers to internal factors that might be less obvious.

By learning about these causes, men can be more prepared. If you spot risk factors in your own life, you can try to reduce their impact. You might not be able to remove all of them, but being aware of them is the first step to making changes. We will also share details that are not often discussed in everyday conversation, which can shed new light on why depression hits so many men.

---

1. Big Life Changes

One of the most common triggers for depression is a major change in life. Examples include divorce, the death of a loved one, retirement, or losing a stable job. These events can make a man question his purpose and place in the world. If a man tied his identity to his job or his role as a husband, losing that role can break his sense of self.

- **Divorce or breakups:** A separation can bring not just heartbreak, but also new living situations and financial struggles. Men might lose daily contact with their children. They might feel guilty about the end of the relationship. These events can weigh heavily on the mind.
- **Loss of a loved one:** Grief is normal, but if it goes on for many months and gets worse, it might turn into depression. Some men feel they must be strong for others, so they never allow themselves to cry or talk about the person they lost.
- **Retirement or job loss:** A job can give structure and a sense of purpose. Without it, men might feel aimless. They might also worry about money. This fear can add to low mood and anxiety.

While big changes can affect anyone, men sometimes deal with them by shutting down or acting out. They might keep it to themselves, leading them to fall deeper into sadness. Recognizing that a life event has thrown you off can help you take the proper steps to handle it.

2. Long-Term Stress

Stress is a normal part of life, but when it becomes chronic, it can lead to depression. Long-term stress wears a person down both mentally and physically. Examples of long-term stress include:

- **High-pressure jobs:** Working in environments where the workload is heavy, deadlines are tight, or the boss is always unhappy can cause a person to live in a constant state of anxiety.
- **Family conflicts:** Ongoing arguments at home, or dealing with a spouse or child who has serious problems, can create a stressful living situation.
- **Financial worries:** Being in debt or struggling to pay bills can lead to a feeling of no escape. Men might feel they have failed as providers, adding shame to the stress.
- **Chronic illness:** When a man or someone in his care has a long-term health condition, it can create constant stress. This stress can be as heavy as the illness itself.

Many men try to fight stress by working harder or ignoring it. Over time, this can lead to burnout. Burnout has many of the same signs as depression: fatigue, low motivation, and irritability. Once burnout sets in, it can be hard to recover without proper rest and changes in daily habits.

---

3. Childhood Trauma or Unresolved Issues

Not all depression starts in adulthood. Some men carry emotional scars from childhood. These could include abuse (physical, emotional, or sexual), neglect, or living in an environment where they never felt safe. A young boy in a household with constant fighting might develop a belief that the world is always hostile. He may carry that belief into adulthood, leading to trust issues or chronic anxiety.

Unresolved issues can sit beneath the surface for years. Men might have flashbacks or nightmares but not connect them to past events. They might have a persistent sense that something is wrong, but not know why. These early experiences can shape the way a man sees himself. He might feel unworthy or fear getting too close to others.

While childhood trauma is not always the sole cause of depression, it can be a strong influence. Therapy or counseling can help uncover these old wounds. Once they come to light, a man can learn healthier ways to handle the pain. This may involve processing the events through talking or specific therapeutic methods. The key is recognizing that the past can affect the present, and that healing is possible with the right steps.

---

4. Underlying Medical Conditions

Sometimes depression is linked to a physical health issue. Medical conditions that cause chronic pain or hormonal changes can raise the risk of depression. For example:

- **Thyroid problems:** An underactive thyroid can cause fatigue, weight gain, and sadness. It can mimic depression. A simple blood test can reveal if thyroid hormones are off balance.
- **Heart disease:** Men with heart problems often experience mood swings or severe worry about their health. This can develop into depression if not addressed.
- **Low testosterone:** Testosterone levels affect energy, mood, and drive. A drop in testosterone can make a man feel sad or apathetic. Checking testosterone levels might help explain some changes in mood.
- **Chronic pain conditions:** Living with unending pain can wear down mental well-being. It can lead to feelings of hopelessness if the pain is poorly managed.

If you suspect a medical issue is fueling your sadness, consult a doctor. A complete checkup can rule out or confirm any physical problems. Addressing the medical condition may ease some depression symptoms. Sometimes, treating an illness can bring new hope. That alone can provide a small boost in mood.

---

5. Substance Use and Unhealthy Coping Methods

Some men try to handle their low mood by drinking alcohol or using other substances. While these might provide brief relief, they often make depression worse in the long run. Alcohol, for example, is a depressant that can affect sleep quality and mood regulation. Over time, a man who drinks heavily might need more and more alcohol to get the same effect, leading to dependence or addiction.

Other unhealthy coping methods include gambling, reckless spending, or engaging in thrill-seeking behavior. These actions can distract from sadness for a short time, but they also come with risks. If a man develops an addiction or faces legal troubles due to his actions, the extra stress can push him further into depression. Recognizing these habits and seeking help early can prevent a spiral that is harder to reverse later.

It is important to note that even substances like certain prescription medications, if misused, can affect mood. Men should be open with their doctors about their substance use, including alcohol and any recreational drugs. A good doctor or counselor will not scold them but will offer safe ways to handle stress and sadness.

---

6. Social Isolation

Humans are social beings. We generally need connection with friends, family, or community groups to maintain good mental health. When a man becomes isolated—whether by choice or by circumstance—he increases his chance of feeling depressed. Isolation can happen gradually. A man might stop hanging out with friends after work. He might turn down invitations because he feels exhausted or uninterested. Over time, these small choices create a lonely life with little support.

Some men isolate themselves due to shame about their situation. They might feel no one can understand them or that their problems will burden others. Isolation can then feed the depression, creating a loop: the more depressed a man feels, the less he wants to be around people, and the lonelier he becomes, which deepens the sadness even more.

Social isolation has a big impact on mental health. Men in particular might not have deep emotional conversations with others. If they lose contact with close friends, they might have no one to turn to. Spotting this pattern early can help. Even small actions—like checking in on a friend or joining a group activity—can reduce the feeling of being alone.

7. Genetics and Family History

If other members of a man's family have struggled with depression, he might be more likely to experience it, too. Genetics play a role in determining a person's vulnerability to mood problems. This does not mean depression is guaranteed, but it raises the possibility. Knowledge of family history can motivate a man to be more aware of changes in his own mood.

Family history can also affect how a man views mental health. If his parents or siblings did not speak about depression, he might believe it is something to keep secret. On the flip side, if there was open communication, he might feel more comfortable seeking help. Genetics is just one factor, but it is important to note. It reminds us that depression is not simply a matter of "effort." Biological factors are often at play.

---

8. Pressure to Meet Social Expectations

Society often gives men certain roles and rules to follow. They might feel obligated to be the main provider in their family, to always be strong, and to never show any signs of sadness. These expectations can be crushing. A man might worry about how others see him. He might spend his entire life trying to meet demands that feel impossible.

This pressure can appear in different forms:

- **Workplace expectations:** Some jobs expect employees to be always on call or ready to deliver results without fail. This can leave little room for rest or emotional health.
- **Cultural norms:** In many cultures, men are taught that crying or admitting fear is wrong. These norms can stop men from reaching out when they need help.
- **Social media:** Images online can show men with perfect bodies, perfect families, and high incomes. Comparing yourself to these images can create feelings of failure or envy.

While healthy ambition can be a good thing, unrealistic demands can push a man toward chronic stress and eventual depression. The key is to see these pressures for what they are—outside forces that do not define a person's worth. Men who learn to question these expectations can lower their emotional strain.

9. Relationship Problems and Conflict

Constant fights with a spouse, partner, or family members can drain a man's emotional energy. This can lead to feelings of hopelessness, especially if he feels he has tried everything to fix the situation. Men might face conflict in:

- **Marriages or partnerships:** Communication breakdowns, lack of intimacy, or serious disagreements about finances can take a toll.
- **Parent-child relationships:** Dealing with rebellious teenagers or children who have special needs can add stress. Men might feel they are failing as fathers.
- **Extended family or in-laws:** Trying to balance many family obligations can be overwhelming. Cultural differences or disagreements about how to manage the household can create tension.

Ongoing conflict can push a man to withdraw or lash out. Either response can add to depression if the root problems are not addressed. Seeking professional help, such as couples counseling or family therapy, can sometimes provide new ways to communicate. If a relationship is truly harmful, ending it might be necessary. But this also needs careful thought, as it can trigger further grief if not handled with caution.

---

10. Bullying or Harassment

Men can face bullying or harassment in different settings, from school to the workplace or online. This can range from threats and insults to more subtle forms of exclusion. Over time, the victim might start believing the negative messages, thinking he deserves the bad treatment. This can lead to deep sadness or a sense of worthlessness.

Workplace harassment is especially common in male-dominated fields where some individuals think toughness should be proved through insults or belittling others. Standing up to bullying can be difficult if a man fears losing his job. However, prolonged bullying can create severe depression. Human resources departments or legal resources can sometimes help.

Online bullying is also on the rise. Hurtful comments on social media can scar a person's self-image. Men might not talk about this issue, feeling it is less serious than in-person bullying. Yet, online attacks can be relentless and cause lasting emotional harm. Recognizing that bullying is not normal can help a man seek the right support, be it from friends, a counselor, or even the police if it becomes threatening.

---

11. Less Obvious Triggers

Not all causes of depression are large and clear. Sometimes small, daily pressures can build up. Examples might include a lengthy commute, dealing with noisy neighbors, or having very little time to rest. These might seem minor, but if they happen every day, they can slowly chip away at a man's mood. Over time, these small stresses can add up to big emotional strain.

Another less obvious factor is seasonal change. Some men experience low mood during colder months, a condition sometimes called seasonal depression. It can happen when there is less sunlight and people spend more time indoors. Making changes to get more natural light, whether through a special lamp or scheduling outdoor time, can help in these cases.

Social comparisons can also be a subtle trigger. A man might see others getting promotions or buying expensive items and feel he is falling behind. If this comparison happens often, it can create a feeling of never being good enough. Identifying these small but persistent triggers can help a man take steps to address them before they fuel deeper depression.

---

12. Combining Causes

Many times, depression comes from a combination of factors. A man might have a genetic tendency toward low mood, plus a stressful job, plus a rocky family life. None of these issues alone might cause full depression, but when they come together, they can become overwhelming. Understanding how several triggers can combine is important. It shows that handling just one cause might not be enough. A multi-step approach is often needed.

For example, a man who lost his job might also have past childhood trauma that makes him fear rejection. If he then withdraws from friends because he feels ashamed, he loses his social support. This kind of chain reaction can lead to severe depression. Untangling these connections can feel challenging, but doing so helps a man see where he can make changes. He might need therapy for the trauma, a practical plan for job searching, and regular time with friends to rebuild his sense of worth.

13. How to Spot Your Own Triggers

Learning to identify causes of depression in your own life can be a key step. Try these simple methods:

- **Write down daily stressors:** Keep a small journal. Each evening, jot down events or thoughts that caused you stress or sadness. Look for patterns.
- **Check your physical health:** If you have had any changes in sleep, appetite, or energy, note these too. Sometimes, physical signs point to hidden depression triggers.
- **Observe your reactions:** When something upsetting happens, do you react with anger, silence, or withdrawal? Knowing your response can reveal which situations hit you hardest.
- **Talk to people you trust:** Sometimes a friend or family member might notice shifts in your behavior before you do. Ask if they have observed anything unusual.

By spotting your triggers, you can act before things get worse. You might need extra rest, a chat with a counselor, or a break from a toxic environment. Addressing the source is usually more helpful than trying to power through it.

---

14. Chapter Summary

Depression in men can arise from many different causes. These include big life changes, chronic stress, childhood trauma, medical conditions, and social pressures. Substance use, isolation, and bullying can also play a role. In many cases, multiple factors combine to push a man toward a low state of mind.

Understanding the common causes can help a man see that his sadness or hopelessness is not random. It is often linked to real life situations or physical conditions. While knowing the cause does not always fix the problem right away, it does point the way to possible solutions. For example, if stress at work is a main trigger, setting clear work boundaries might help. If low testosterone levels are part of the problem, a visit to a doctor might bring relief.

In the upcoming chapters, we will talk about warning signs, symptoms, and the ways men can handle their sadness before it grows. We will also explore why many men hide their feelings and how to break that pattern. With the basics of causes and triggers in mind, men can start to see that depression is not an unsolvable puzzle. By focusing on specific factors, each person can begin to form a plan to move toward better mental health.

CHAPTER 3: WARNING SIGNS AND SYMPTOMS

Depression can sometimes grow without a man noticing the shift in his mood or daily habits. Men might dismiss early signs, thinking they are just having a bad week or that stress is normal. When these warning signs are not addressed, they can worsen, affecting relationships, jobs, and health. In this chapter, we will look closely at both common and less recognized symptoms that indicate a deeper low mood. This can help men decide when it is time to seek support.

We will explore mental, physical, and behavioral clues. We will also talk about ways to see these clues in yourself and in the men around you. Men often assume they must push through, but seeing the problem early can prevent many long-term troubles. If you notice these signs in your own life, it does not mean you are weak. It means your body and mind are telling you something important.

---

1. Clear Mood-Related Symptoms

A central warning sign of depression is a low, sad, or empty mood. Many men do feel sadness, but they do not always share it openly. They might also feel hopeless, as if nothing will ever improve. Some men can experience a sense of guilt for no obvious reason, or a constant worry that they are failing at life.

- **Persistent sadness:** This is not just feeling sad for a day or two; it lasts for weeks or months.
- **Loss of interest:** Men might stop caring about sports, hobbies, or social events that once mattered to them.
- **Feeling worthless:** A man may have thoughts that he is no good to anyone, or that his life lacks purpose.

This cluster of mood changes often shows up in subtle ways. Perhaps a man starts putting off tasks he once did happily. He may skip outings with friends. He may also feel more negativity in general, even toward things that do not usually upset him. These shifts might seem minor at first, but when they continue for a while, they point to something deeper than ordinary sadness.

---

2. Anger and Irritability

Men sometimes show their low mood through anger or annoyance, rather than crying or talking about sadness. This anger can appear in many situations, such as a small disagreement at home or a minor frustration at work. The intensity of the anger might shock even the man himself.

- **Frequent outbursts:** Shouting or picking fights over things that seem small to others.
- **Frustration with daily life:** Feeling that everything is a source of stress, from traffic jams to a long line at the store.
- **Blaming others or the world:** A sense that everyone is against you, leading to aggressive thoughts or words.

This anger may push people away. Friends or family might be uncertain how to help. They see the anger but do not realize it could be depression. For men who feel ashamed or guilty about their sadness, anger can be a shield. It keeps the real issue hidden. Learning to notice when anger is tied to deeper sadness can be an important step toward finding relief.

---

3. Physical Warning Signs

Depression does not just affect thoughts; it can also show up in the body. Men might notice aches, tiredness, or changes in appetite. They could visit the doctor for headaches or stomach problems, never suspecting that these might be connected to a mental state.

- **Ongoing fatigue:** Feeling drained, no matter how much sleep you get. This tiredness might make tasks at work or home feel bigger and more daunting.
- **Sleep changes:** Struggling to fall asleep or waking up too early and not being able to get back to sleep. Some men might sleep much more than usual, using rest as an escape.
- **Appetite changes:** This could be eating far more or much less than before. It can result in weight gain or weight loss that seems sudden.
- **Unexplained pain:** Backaches, headaches, or digestive problems with no clear physical cause.

These physical symptoms can sometimes lead to more frustration, especially if medical tests do not uncover a clear reason. It can be difficult for a man to accept that his body aches might come from ongoing sadness or stress. However, once a medical cause is ruled out, it is wise to consider the possibility that depression might be a factor.

4. Changes in Thinking and Focus

Depression can also affect the way a man thinks. He might notice that his mind feels foggy or slow. Tasks that used to be simple, such as responding to emails or planning the day, become harder. He might have difficulty remembering things or making decisions.

- **Trouble concentrating:** A man might read the same page of a book several times and still not understand it. At work, he might miss important points during meetings.
- **Memory lapses:** Forgetting deadlines, special dates, or everyday tasks. It might feel like the brain is stuck in mud.
- **Negative self-talk:** Repeated thoughts of being a failure or never doing anything right. This can happen automatically, without any real proof.

These thinking changes can affect job performance or cause conflicts with friends and family. It can be confusing to see one's thinking skills slip, especially if one has always been mentally sharp. Men might try to hide these lapses, fearing it will look like they are not capable. Recognizing the link between foggy thinking and depression can lessen shame and guide men to proper help.

5. Social Withdrawal

Another key sign is pulling away from people. Men with depression often stop calling friends, skip social events, or isolate themselves in other ways. They might spend hours alone with video games, or they might avoid answering their phones. While alone time can sometimes be helpful for rest, constant withdrawal can deepen the low mood.

- **Declining invites:** A man might say he is too busy or too tired to go out. Over time, friends might stop asking.

- **Lack of interest in conversation:** Even when physically present, he might not engage much in talk. He might sit quietly, giving short answers.
- **Staying home instead of seeking fun:** Activities that used to be appealing might feel like they take too much energy.

Social withdrawal can become a cycle. The more isolated a man becomes, the lonelier he feels. That loneliness then feeds the depression. It is important to notice if you or a loved one is pulling away in ways that are out of character.

---

6. Risky or Reckless Behavior

Some men with depression turn to dangerous actions as a way to cope or escape. This might include driving too fast, getting into physical fights, or gambling large sums of money. In some cases, it can also mean turning to drugs or alcohol more frequently. While these activities might briefly distract from sadness, they usually bring more problems.

- **Increased substance use:** Drinking more alcohol than usual, using drugs, or mixing different substances.
- **Spending sprees:** Blowing large amounts of money on items not needed or betting big on gambling.
- **Reckless physical acts:** Doing stunts, extreme sports without safety measures, or driving in an aggressive way.

Such behavior can be a clue that a man feels he has little to lose. It might also be a hidden attempt to test boundaries or punish himself. If you find yourself or someone you care about engaging in more reckless actions, ask if there might be an underlying sadness that is fueling those choices.

---

7. Unusual Changes in Personal Habits

Men might start neglecting their personal hygiene or daily routine when depression sets in. Taking a shower, brushing teeth, or changing clothes regularly can feel like too much work. They might also lose track of chores or errands. The fridge might be empty because shopping feels overwhelming. Rooms might stay messy for weeks.

On the other hand, some men might go the opposite direction, obsessively cleaning or focusing on small tasks to avoid thinking about their sadness. They might spend all day rearranging items or doing yard work to block out negative thoughts. Either extreme—neglect or over-focus—can be a sign that something deeper is happening.

8. Thoughts of Giving Up

One of the most severe signs of depression is thinking that life is not worth living. This can take the form of passive thoughts like, "It would be better if I wasn't here," or more active ideas about harming oneself. Some men might not talk about these thoughts at all, so it is difficult for friends or family to notice.

- **Feeling trapped:** A man might believe there is no way out of his current problems.
- **Fixation on death:** This might include writing letters, giving away prized items, or talking about death in a casual or "joking" manner.
- **Planning self-harm:** Thinking of specific ways to hurt oneself or gathering items to do so.

These signs need immediate attention. If you see them in yourself or someone else, it is vital to reach out to a mental health hotline or a trusted person. Many men feel intense shame about these thoughts, but sharing them with a professional can prevent a tragic outcome.

9. Less Recognized Signs

Not all signs of depression are obvious. Sometimes the clues are subtle or might overlap with other conditions. Here are a few examples:

- **Sexual problems:** A drop in drive or finding no joy in physical closeness can be a clue. Some medications or stress conditions also affect this, but depression can be a major reason as well.
- **OCD-like behaviors:** Repetitive rituals might appear, like checking doors many times or washing hands often. This does not always mean a man has a separate condition; it might be a sign of severe anxiety linked to depression.

- **Getting lost in work:** Working very late or focusing on the job might look like ambition. But if it is a drastic change, it could be an effort to avoid personal problems.
- **Numbing out with media:** Watching endless hours of TV, scrolling through social media, or playing video games for a long time can be a way to ignore low mood.

These less recognized signs might not fit the typical picture of a sad person. They still point to a deeper emotional state that needs attention.

10. Recognizing Patterns Over Time

One bad day or a few tense weeks do not always mean a person is depressed. Depression usually involves ongoing patterns lasting at least a couple of weeks, often longer. If you notice a cluster of these signs for a month or more, it is time to pay attention. People often assume they will snap out of it, but persistent low mood is a serious sign.

A useful practice is to note changes in your daily habits or overall outlook. If you see a downward trend, try to check in with yourself or talk to someone. Sometimes an outside perspective from a friend, partner, or counselor can help you see the pattern you have missed.

11. How to Distinguish Depression from Normal Stress

Normal stress can cause temporary sadness or tiredness, but it usually passes once the situation improves. Depression, on the other hand, continues even when life seems calm on the outside. You might succeed at work or fix a personal conflict, yet still feel a lingering heaviness.

Men sometimes say, "I'm just busy," when in fact their motivation is gone and they have no sense of enjoyment. They might blame a rough patch at work, but the mood does not lift even after the work slows down. When sadness remains long after stress should have ended, it suggests a deeper issue.

12. Observing These Signs in Friends or Family

It is not always easy to see depression in another man, especially if he hides his feelings well. However, you might notice certain clues:

- **Behavior changes:** Maybe he used to be active but now sits around doing nothing. Or perhaps he used to make jokes and now is quiet.
- **Avoiding social events:** If a friend who loved hanging out has vanished, that might be a red flag.
- **Talk of hopelessness:** Phrases like "There's no point," or "Why bother?" might signal depressed thinking.

If you see these signs, consider reaching out gently. Try not to shame or judge. You can say, "I've noticed you don't seem yourself lately. Want to talk about it?" Simple words can open a door. He might not respond right away, but at least he knows someone cares and is willing to listen.

---

13. The Cost of Ignoring the Warning Signs

Men who ignore these signs can face bigger problems. Depression can affect work performance, leading to poor reviews or job loss. It can weaken relationships, causing breakups or strained ties with children. Unchecked depression can also lead to substance use or unhealthy coping. In the worst cases, it can lead to self-harm.

Physical health might suffer too. Chronic depression has been linked to higher chances of heart problems, headaches, or immunity issues. The longer a man waits to address these symptoms, the harder it might be to recover fully. Early action can prevent deeper fallout.

---

14. Checking In with Yourself

Men sometimes rush through their days without pausing to see how they feel. Regular check-ins can help spot warning signs early. Set aside a few moments each day, maybe before bed, to ask yourself how you are feeling emotionally and physically. Note if you feel more tension, sadness, or numbness than usual. Are you dreading the next day? Are you angry for no clear reason?

You could track these feelings on a simple chart or in a journal. If you notice a trend over several weeks, consider talking to someone about it. This could be a close friend, a counselor, or a medical professional.

15. Small Tests to Measure Your Mood

There are short questionnaires you can take that measure your level of sadness or anxious feelings. These are not meant to diagnose you by themselves, but they can provide hints. For instance, some doctors use a scale of questions that ask about interest in activities, appetite, sleep, and thoughts about daily life. Scoring high suggests you might need further evaluation.

If you prefer not to see a professional right away, you can find some basic checklists online. However, be cautious about self-diagnosing. The best course is to see a trained person if you suspect any signs. An expert can consider your full situation and suggest a path that fits your needs.

16. Practical Steps if You See These Signs

If you recognize multiple signs of depression in yourself or someone else, take the following steps:

1. **Talk to a trusted person:** This could be a friend, partner, or family member. Share a few details about how you feel. You do not have to reveal everything at once.
2. **Seek professional input:** A doctor can rule out physical causes. A mental health specialist can help confirm if it is depression and advise on possible treatments.
3. **Consider lifestyle changes:** Look at your diet, exercise habits, and sleep routines. Even small improvements in these areas can ease some symptoms.
4. **Check your environment:** If your job or living situation is severely draining, think about changes. Sometimes adjusting your environment can reduce stress.
5. **Avoid hiding:** If you keep these warning signs to yourself, you risk letting them deepen. Reaching out is an important step in preventing a crisis.

These actions might feel scary, but they can stop a downward spiral. Remember that many men have gone through similar experiences and found helpful methods to manage them.

17. Chapter Summary

In this chapter, we discussed many clues that show up when a man is experiencing depression. These range from clear mood issues and physical aches to less obvious signs like anger, social withdrawal, and reckless habits. We also looked at how to tell the difference between normal stress and a deeper, more lasting sadness.

Noticing early signs of low mood in yourself or a friend can be life-changing. Rather than seeing these signs as a personal flaw, it is better to see them as alerts that something needs to be addressed. Seeking help early can save jobs, relationships, and well-being.

In the next chapter, we will focus on **why men tend to hide their feelings**. We will explore how cultural expectations, family backgrounds, and personal fears contribute to a pattern of silence. Recognizing this pattern is key to moving beyond it and discovering new ways to handle low mood and sadness.

CHAPTER 4: WHY MEN HIDE THEIR FEELINGS

Many men face a strong impulse to keep their low mood or stress hidden. This pattern often starts early in life and can be reinforced by messages from family, peers, and society. By looking at why men feel compelled to lock away their emotions, we can understand how to break this habit. When men learn to share and seek help instead of staying silent, they often find healthier ways to handle sadness.

In this chapter, we will explore factors such as social norms, fear of judgment, and the pressure to appear strong. We will also look at the damage that silence can do, both mentally and physically. By shining a light on these hidden feelings, men can recognize that speaking about their worries is not a sign of weakness. It is a sign of responsibility to oneself and to those who care about us.

---

1. Early Lessons About Masculinity

From a young age, many boys are taught to be tough. They might hear messages like "don't cry," or "boys don't show weakness." These lessons can become so internalized that men feel shame when they sense tears or sadness. Some families never talk about emotional pain, creating an atmosphere where any sign of distress seems abnormal.

- **Learning to be silent:** If a boy is told to stop crying whenever he is upset, he might decide that sharing sadness is wrong. This can become second nature by adulthood.
- **Pressure from peers:** In school or on sports teams, boys might tease those who show vulnerability. This can be a powerful incentive to keep quiet.
- **Modeling from father figures:** If a father or male guardian never showed emotion, the child may copy that pattern later in life.

These early lessons do not simply vanish with age. Instead, they shape how men handle stress, loss, and conflict. Many men grow into adulthood believing they must hide any sign of emotional trouble. This can lead to bottled-up feelings that eventually push them toward harmful behaviors.

---

2. Fear of Judgment

Men often worry about what friends, coworkers, or partners will think if they admit to sadness or anxiety. They might fear being labeled as weak, unstable, or not fit to lead. This fear can be especially strong in workplaces that value confidence and determination above all else.

- **Concern about job security:** A man might think that showing vulnerability at work could harm his standing or career advancement. He worries that coworkers will see him differently.
- **Romantic relationships:** Some men fear their partner will lose respect for them if they talk about not feeling well mentally. They might worry their partner will see them as a burden.
- **Male friend groups:** Men might think their friends will not know how to react or will tease them. This is often based on the idea that men should keep emotional talk to a minimum.

In reality, many people respond with sympathy when someone is honest about feeling low. But if a man has seen or heard negative reactions before, he might assume that will be the norm. These fears, whether true or imagined, can form a strong barrier to reaching out.

---

3. The Provider Role

Many men see themselves as the family provider. They think they must hold it together for others, whether that is a spouse, children, or aging parents. In this role, any sign of low mood can feel like letting the family down. A man might think, "I need to be the rock here. I can't show that I'm not okay."

- **Financial stress:** A man might believe that if he admits he is struggling, it could signal that the family's stability is at risk.
- **Handling big decisions:** Men may feel a duty to make key choices about the family's future, and they fear that showing stress could undermine confidence in those decisions.
- **Hiding worries from children:** Fathers might avoid talking about sadness so their kids do not worry. They believe silence is the best way to keep the household calm.

While caring for loved ones is honorable, always hiding problems can backfire. Children sometimes sense when a father is upset, and not talking about it can create confusion or tension in the home. It can also increase a man's stress if he never gets the support he needs.

4. Avoiding Embarrassment

A common reason men stay silent is embarrassment. They might feel uneasy describing tears or deep sadness. Talking about personal trauma or anxious thoughts can feel awkward. Some men have never practiced putting emotional experiences into words, so they do not know how to begin.

- **Lack of vocabulary:** Men might only know a few words to describe their state, like "fine" or "stressed." They might not be used to naming emotions like guilt, worry, or sorrow.
- **Fear of getting it wrong:** They might worry about stumbling over words or not making sense when trying to explain their feelings.
- **Shame over not being able to fix themselves:** Men often feel they should have all the answers. Admitting they do not can be uncomfortable.

Yet, learning to talk about these issues is a skill, just like any other. It takes time to practice. Opening up to a counselor or a close friend can be a first step to getting more comfortable. Overcoming embarrassment can lead to deeper connections and better understanding from those around you.

5. The Influence of Media and Pop Culture

Movies, TV shows, and social media often display strong male figures who rarely show sadness. Men are usually shown as heroes or action stars who solve problems on their own. When men see these examples repeatedly, they might think that is how they should be in real life too.

- **Fear of not measuring up:** If a man believes he should be as calm and fearless as a fictional character, he might see himself as lacking.
- **Reinforced stereotypes:** Comments from others such as, "Be a man" or "Tough it out," tie in with what is shown in the media.
- **Social media comparisons:** Men might see other men posting cheerful updates, success stories, and fitness milestones. They might feel alone if they are struggling.

In truth, media images often leave out the reality that real men face ups and downs. Feeling sad or anxious is part of being human. Acknowledging that pop culture may not be showing the whole story can help men realize that they are not defective if they have low moods.

6. Denial of Vulnerability

Denial is one of the most powerful forces keeping men silent. A man might tell himself, "I'm just tired," or "It's just a busy time." He might deny that anything is truly wrong. This can go on for months or years. The root cause is often the belief that acknowledging depression is the same as being weak.

- **Ignoring physical clues:** Even if a man has headaches, stomachaches, or trouble sleeping, he might not connect it to a deeper emotional issue.
- **Refusing to talk:** When friends or family ask if something is bothering him, he quickly says, "No, I'm fine," to shut down the conversation.
- **Convincing himself he is not depressed:** Some men genuinely do not believe they can have depression, because they think it only looks a certain way.

Breaking through denial means accepting that feeling depressed does not make someone less of a man. It is an issue that affects the mind and body. Just like any other health concern, it needs proper attention.

7. The Downside of "Stoic" Approaches

Stoicism is sometimes seen as a noble trait: the ability to stay calm under pressure. While it can be helpful in certain situations, constant stoicism can lead to bottled-up emotions. If a man never releases or processes his feelings, they can build up and cause a breakdown later.

- **Overemphasis on self-reliance:** A man might be proud of handling problems alone. But some problems, like deep sadness, might need expert help or at least a listening ear.
- **Misunderstanding stoicism:** True stoicism does not mean ignoring one's emotions. It means learning to manage them in a balanced way. Many men interpret it as shutting down all feeling.

- **Emotional numbness:** The man might reach a point where he does not feel much of anything, good or bad. This numbness can be a sign of severe depression.

While a calm approach to stress can be good, complete emotional shutdown is harmful. It can make the man feel lonely and stop others from knowing what is truly going on.

---

8. Family and Cultural Taboos

Some cultures place great emphasis on a man's role as a pillar of strength. In these settings, there might be little understanding of mental health issues. Men might be told that seeing a counselor is only for people with serious mental problems. They might also be warned not to show any sign of sadness or worry.

- **Shame or ridicule:** In some families, men who mention feeling down might be told to "get over it" or be laughed at.
- **Pressure from religious or traditional views:** Men might believe it is their duty to remain strong and unwavering for the family's sake.
- **Fear of losing respect:** There might be a real concern that others in the community or extended family will gossip if a man speaks openly about his struggles.

These taboos can stop men from even considering help. They might see it as violating tradition or letting their family down. Yet, mental health problems can occur in any culture or social group. Finding a trusted person within the community or seeking private help can be a way to navigate these taboos without making a big public statement.

---

9. The Effect on Physical Health

Hiding feelings does not just affect the mind; it can also harm the body. Ongoing stress can raise blood pressure, harm sleep, and weaken the immune system. Some men keep quiet until they experience a heart scare or other major health issue. Even then, they might not connect the dots to their unspoken sadness.

- **Increased stress hormones:** When a man pretends everything is fine, his body might continue releasing stress hormones. This can lead to tension headaches or digestive problems.

- **Unhealthy coping:** Bottling emotions sometimes drives a man to drink more, smoke, or eat in unhealthy ways to manage the unspoken stress.
- **Delayed medical care:** A man might avoid the doctor because he does not want to appear worried. By the time he seeks help, problems may have gotten worse.

Seeing the link between emotional silence and physical health can motivate men to open up. Looking after mental health is an important part of looking after the body.

---

10. Relationship Problems

When men keep their worries hidden, it can strain their relationships. Partners might sense that something is wrong but feel shut out. Conflicts can arise because of mood swings or frustration that the man does not explain.

- **Lack of communication:** Hiding sadness prevents honest talk. The partner might mistake the man's silence for disinterest or anger directed at them.
- **Resentment building:** The man might grow bitter that nobody understands him, even though he never shares what he is feeling.
- **Emotional distance:** Over time, the gap might widen until intimacy and trust suffer. The partner might feel alone, despite being in a relationship.

Even close friendships can fade if men do not share real emotions. Friends might feel the man is distant or aloof. By talking openly, men can keep connections strong and gain a support system that helps them through tough times.

---

11. Work-Related Consequences

In many jobs, men might worry that admitting to sadness will hurt their position. They might think their boss or coworkers will see them as unstable or unfit for leadership roles. As a result, they stay quiet and let the stress pile up.

- **Errors at work:** A mind weighed down by unspoken worries can lead to mistakes or missed deadlines.
- **Reduced creativity:** Constantly holding in emotions can sap energy and block new ideas.

- **Burnout risk:** Bottled-up stress can accelerate burnout. This is a state of deep exhaustion that can force a person to quit or take a long leave.

In some workplaces, there are employee assistance programs or mental health days. Men might be hesitant to use these, fearing judgment. Yet those who do use them can find relief and return to work with better focus. Employers often prefer an employee who seeks help rather than one who silently struggles and eventually leaves the job.

12. Missing Out on Support

One of the saddest outcomes of hiding feelings is that men miss out on support that might help them recover faster. Friends and family often want to help but cannot if they do not know what is happening.

- **Practical help:** Loved ones might take on some responsibilities or offer resources if they knew a man was overwhelmed.
- **Emotional support:** Talking to someone who cares can ease the heaviness of sadness. Sharing worries can reduce their power.
- **Professional guidance:** Doctors, therapists, or counselors can provide proven ways to handle low mood, but a man first needs to admit he needs assistance.

By staying silent, men do not give others the chance to help. They might also deny themselves the chance to learn from professionals who have guided many people through similar troubles.

13. Real-Life Examples of Openness

Although there is a widespread pattern of men hiding their feelings, some men do choose to speak up. Those who do often find that their relationships improve. They might even discover new closeness with family and friends. Others report that seeking therapy or talking openly helped them save their jobs, marriages, or even their lives.

These men might say they were scared at first. Perhaps they thought no one would understand. But many times, they found people were more open-minded than expected. Their stories remind us that there is a real benefit in breaking the silence.

14. How to Start Sharing

For men who have never opened up, the idea of talking about sadness can feel overwhelming. Here are some tips:

1. **Start small:** Share a bit of your feelings with one person you trust. You do not have to lay out every detail right away.
2. **Write it down first:** If speaking is hard, try writing a short note or email to someone you trust. This can help organize your thoughts.
3. **Pick the right time and place:** Choose a private, calm setting to avoid interruptions. This helps reduce the pressure you might feel.
4. **Seek professional help first:** Sometimes a counselor is the easiest place to start because they are trained to handle emotional discussions. You do not have to worry about burdening them.

Once you have taken a small step, the next steps might feel less scary. You will likely discover that most people do not see you as weak for sharing. In fact, they may respect your honesty and care about helping.

---

15. Using Technology to Break the Ice

In today's world, men might find it easier to begin talking about low mood through digital tools. This can be through online forums, support chat rooms, or messaging apps. Communicating in writing can help remove some of the embarrassment or fear of judgment. Men can connect with others who have similar experiences, even if they live far away.

- **Anonymous chats:** Some websites let you speak without giving your real name. This can be a good first step if you feel uneasy about revealing your identity.
- **Apps for mental health:** There are apps that provide exercises, mood tracking, and tips. Sharing progress in an online group can also build a sense of community.
- **Virtual therapy sessions:** Some therapists offer online video meetings. This can be more comfortable for a man who does not want to visit a physical office.

These modern options might remove one barrier to sharing. However, face-to-face contact still plays a big role in building trust and support in the real world. The key is to pick a method that works best for you.

16. The Cost of Always Appearing "Strong"

When men are always trying to look strong, they can lose contact with their genuine feelings. They might appear confident, but on the inside, they are stressed or full of self-doubt. Over time, this disconnect can create a split between the outer image and the inner reality.

- **Emotional exhaustion:** Holding up a strong front uses a lot of energy. This can leave a man too tired to handle normal tasks.
- **Missed connections:** Others might see the man as distant and not try to connect. He loses the chance for closeness or real friendship.
- **Sudden emotional crashes:** If a man holds everything inside, he can snap when pressure gets too high. This could show up as rage, panic, or a breakdown.

Admitting that you do not always feel strong can actually strengthen your bond with others. It lets them see you as a real person, not a flawless facade. Authentic connections are often built on sharing both good times and bad.

---

17. Chapter Summary

Many men hide their feelings due to social lessons, fear of judgment, and the desire to appear strong. The world often reinforces the idea that men should not talk about sadness or worry. But this silence can cause real harm. It can lead to broken relationships, poor physical health, and a deeper form of depression that is harder to address.

Learning to talk about problems does not mean you stop being strong. Instead, it shows you care about your well-being and respect the people who rely on you. Though it may be difficult at first, opening up can bring relief and prevent worse outcomes. It is possible to balance strength with honesty, showing that men, like anyone else, deserve help when facing low mood.

In the next two chapters, we will focus on **breaking harmful habits** and **helpful tools for the mind**. We will go through specific actions and strategies that men can use to break free from destructive patterns and start building mental health practices that truly work. By understanding why men hide their feelings, we can take steps to create a healthier and more open future.

CHAPTER 5: BREAKING HARMFUL HABITS

Men who deal with ongoing sadness often end up with habits that add more stress or make them feel worse. These habits can include abusing alcohol, spending too much time on electronic devices, or avoiding problems that need attention. In this chapter, we will look at ways to spot and break these harmful routines. We will also discuss effective methods to prevent them from returning later.

Breaking an unhelpful habit is more than just stopping a certain activity. It involves examining the thoughts and triggers that lead to the behavior. By learning how to replace harmful habits with better ones, men can create healthier daily patterns and protect their mental well-being.

---

1. How Bad Habits Take Root

Many harmful habits start as a quick fix for dealing with stress, sadness, or anxiety. A man might drink alcohol to numb difficult feelings or skip exercise because he feels too drained to move. At first, these small choices may not seem like a big deal. But if they turn into regular patterns, they can affect health and mood over time.

- **Avoiding tasks:** Putting off important tasks might feel good short term. It removes that immediate worry. Yet, over time, deadlines pile up, stress grows, and self-esteem drops.
- **Escaping with technology:** It is easy to watch hours of videos or play online games to forget about sadness. But this can lead to social isolation or poor sleep if it goes on too long.
- **Excessive substance use:** Men might turn to alcohol, cigarettes, or other substances to cope with pressure. In the long run, these can damage the body and deepen the sadness.

A person might ask, "Why don't I just stop?" But habits are deeply wired into our behavior. The brain likes shortcuts, and once it learns that a certain action brings quick relief or distraction, it will repeat it. That is why we must look at the triggers, motives, and hidden rewards behind any habit we want to break.

---

2. Recognizing Warning Signs in Your Routine

Men who want to improve their mental state should look carefully at their daily routine. Sometimes these routines might include small actions that, if repeated, harm the mind or body. Recognizing these actions is the first step to removing them.

- **Repeated negative thoughts:** Telling yourself, "I'm a failure" or "I'm not good enough," whenever you make a mistake. This self-talk often becomes an automatic habit.
- **Physical neglect:** Skipping regular meals, drinking too many sugary drinks, or getting little physical activity. Over time, these choices sap energy and lower mood.
- **Emotional outbursts:** Anger or outbursts in response to small annoyances can be a habit. It can push others away and create guilt or shame afterward.
- **Late-night phone use:** Staying up to read negative news or scroll social media can ruin sleep, making it easier to feel low or irritable the next day.

To spot these kinds of habits, keep a short log for a week. Write down anything you do every day that makes you feel worse afterward. At the end of the week, you will have a clear view of the top areas you should target.

---

3. Replacing Bad Habits Instead of Just Stopping Them

One of the most common mistakes men make is trying to quit a bad habit with no plan to fill the gap. Habits usually provide something, even if it is destructive in the long run. For example, if a man turns to video games every night, he might be seeking comfort, distraction, or a sense of accomplishment. If he simply quits gaming without finding a better activity, he might feel empty and return to the old habit.

- **Identify the need:** Is the habit meeting a need to relax, distract, or feel good about yourself? This is often the hidden reward.
- **Find a better replacement:** If a man is using alcohol to calm down after work, he might replace that with a brisk walk, some quiet reading, or a healthy snack. This new action must also satisfy the need to decompress, but without the same risks.

- **Track progress:** Keep a simple chart. Each time you avoid the old habit and do the new one, make a note. Rewards, like telling yourself "Good job" or taking a short break, can reinforce the new behavior.

Replacing a habit takes time. The brain needs repeated practice to prefer the new behavior over the old one. During this period, slip-ups can happen. Instead of quitting after a slip, see it as a learning moment. Try to figure out what triggered the slip and plan how to respond differently next time.

---

4. Breaking the Cycle of Procrastination

Procrastination is very common among men who feel sad or overwhelmed. Tasks seem too big, so they decide to wait, hoping to feel more prepared later. This creates a cycle of guilt, stress, and even more sadness when deadlines loom or important matters are not handled.

Key steps to beat procrastination:

1. **Set small tasks:** If the overall task looks huge, break it into smaller actions. For example, if you need to organize your home office, pick one drawer or shelf at a time.
2. **Time limits:** Use a simple timer. Work on a task for 10 or 20 minutes without distraction. You can take a short pause after. Often, getting started is the hardest part.
3. **Visual reminders:** Use sticky notes or a phone calendar to remind yourself what needs to be done. Cross off tasks when finished. Seeing progress builds momentum.
4. **Accountability buddy:** Find a friend or coworker who also wants to reduce procrastination. Check in once a day or once a week to share progress. Encouragement can be powerful.

When men stop putting off tasks, they often feel a boost in mood. Completing even small items can create a sense of success. Over time, this helps build self-esteem and reduces the feeling of being stuck.

5. Handling Anger and Conflict Without Toxic Patterns

Anger can become a harmful habit if a man constantly yells or lashes out whenever he faces stress. This behavior can damage relationships and create more guilt or shame. Learning healthy ways to handle anger is a major step toward better mental health.

- **Pause before reacting:** When you feel anger rising, count slowly to five or even ten. This brief pause can prevent an immediate outburst and give you time to choose a calmer response.
- **Learn to listen:** During conflicts, a man might focus on defending himself. Instead, practice listening to the other person's viewpoint. This can reduce misunderstandings that fuel anger.
- **Use "I" statements:** Say, "I feel upset when..." rather than accusing the other person with "You always..." or "You never..." This can stop the conflict from getting worse.
- **Identify triggers:** Some topics, like money or work pressure, might trigger bigger anger responses. Knowing these triggers can help you plan calmer ways to handle them.

Anger itself is not always bad. It can show that something matters deeply to you. But the habit of letting anger dictate your actions can hurt your mental health. Replacing uncontrolled anger with healthier communication reduces stress and lifts some of the emotional weight on your mind.

---

6. Less Obvious Harmful Habits

There are some habits men might not realize are harmful because they seem harmless at first:

- **Perfectionism:** Always aiming for absolute perfection can lead to constant stress and a fear of failure. Men with perfectionist habits often postpone tasks or never finish them.
- **Self-blame:** If you catch yourself taking the blame for everything, even when it is not your fault, this can create a pattern of constant guilt. Over time, it eats away at self-confidence.
- **Over-apologizing:** Saying "I'm sorry" for every small thing can become a habit. It might signal deeper issues of low self-worth or a need for approval.

- **Chronic comparison:** Constantly comparing yourself to friends, coworkers, or social media images can create envy or sadness. It can become a daily habit to measure your life against others.

Once you name a habit, you can work on changing it. This can involve small mindset adjustments. For example, practice saying "I did my best" instead of chasing perfection every time. Or choose to celebrate little steps instead of looking at what others are doing.

---

7. Building Boundaries to Protect Your Progress

Breaking harmful habits requires a supportive environment. If you keep people or situations around that push you toward those habits, you might struggle. Setting boundaries involves deciding what you will and will not allow in your life.

- **Social boundaries:** If a friend always encourages you to over-drink or engage in risky behaviors, you might need to limit your time with them. Or you can discuss your new goals and see if they respect them.
- **Work boundaries:** If your job demands that you stay late every day, leading to burnout and harmful coping methods, it may be time to talk to your supervisor about realistic work hours.
- **Digital boundaries:** Limit phone use after a certain hour or remove apps that trap you for hours without real benefit. Setting phone-free times can be very helpful for mental rest.

Boundaries protect the progress you are making. They reduce the amount of stress and temptation around you. Men often find that once they set basic boundaries, it becomes easier to stick to healthier behaviors.

---

8. Reward Systems That Work

The human brain responds to rewards. When trying to replace or break habits, men sometimes forget to give themselves healthy rewards for doing well. This reward should not be something that puts you back into a negative cycle. Instead, choose small treats or experiences that do not harm your mind or body.

- **Short breaks:** If you finish a task you have been avoiding, give yourself 15 minutes of guilt-free relaxation. Use it to read, sit quietly, or do something you find peaceful.

- **Social rewards:** Plan a simple activity with a friend or loved one once you reach a certain goal, like going for a casual walk or having a simple meal together.
- **Personal tokens:** Some men wear a small bracelet or keep a coin in their pocket to remind themselves of a goal. Each time they look at it, they feel a little boost.

Rewards do not have to be large or expensive. The key is to link positive actions to a sense of satisfaction or pride. Over time, the habit of making better choices will become part of daily life without needing constant reminders.

9. Handling Slip-Ups Wisely

Nobody breaks a harmful habit perfectly on the first try. There will likely be days when you backslide or fail to keep a new routine. The danger is in labeling yourself a failure and giving up. A slip-up is an event, not a definition of who you are.

- **Review the trigger:** Ask yourself what caused the slip-up. Was it stress at work, boredom, or an argument at home?
- **Plan a change:** Once you know the trigger, decide how to handle that situation next time. Maybe you need a short walk instead of reaching for a drink, or you need to text a friend instead of shutting down.
- **Self-compassion:** Treat yourself with kindness. If you beat yourself up mentally, it can push you deeper into negative habits. Recognize that everyone makes mistakes when changing behavior.

Over time, slip-ups should become less frequent and less severe. Each time you recover from a mistake, you get a bit stronger and more aware of how to manage triggers.

10. Handling Relationships That Encourage Bad Habits

Sometimes, the hardest part of changing your behavior is dealing with people in your life who do not support your changes. This might be a friend who always wants to party late, or a family member who belittles your efforts to improve yourself.

- **Open communication:** Tell them you are trying to stop or replace a certain habit. Explain that you would appreciate their support or at least their respect.
- **Offer alternatives:** If a friend wants to meet at a bar, suggest a simpler place or a coffee shop. If they insist on the bar, set a limit on how long you will stay.
- **Know your limits:** If someone keeps pushing you to do what you are trying to avoid, it may be necessary to spend less time with them. This can be tough, but your mental health is important.
- **Seek out supportive groups:** Try to find new friends or groups who share healthier interests. This can include sports clubs, local volunteer activities, or online groups focused on positive habits.

The company you keep has a strong influence on your daily choices. While you might not always be able to change those around you, you can control how you respond to them and how often you are in tempting environments.

---

11. A Closer Look at Unhealthy Escape Methods

Men might lean on methods that seem harmless but become big problems over time. Here are a few examples and why they can be harmful:

- **Eating for comfort:** A man might turn to high-calorie snacks or sugary foods to push away sad feelings. This can lead to weight gain and guilt, which then deepens low mood.
- **Endless scrolling:** Men can spend hours reading news or browsing social media. This can create a pattern of comparing oneself to others, leading to envy or self-criticism.
- **Excessive shopping:** Buying things you do not need can drain your finances and pile up debt. It may give a short "rush" but leaves you with regret afterward.
- **Keeping too busy:** Some men hide their sadness by working very long hours or cramming their schedule. While this might look productive, it can keep them from confronting deeper issues.

Recognizing these patterns of escape is a critical step. Often, they look normal from the outside. But if they are repeated often to avoid facing sadness, they can lead to bigger mental or financial troubles later.

12. Building Self-Awareness for Lasting Change

A good way to prevent falling back into harmful habits is to increase your self-awareness. This involves checking in with your emotions and thoughts throughout the day. By spotting stress or sadness early, you can choose a healthy response before the impulse to do something harmful grows too strong.

- **Quick self-checks:** A few times a day, pause to ask, "How am I feeling right now? What do I need at this moment?" This can be as brief as 30 seconds.
- **Mindful breathing:** When tension rises, try taking slow, deep breaths. Focus on the breath. This can help calm the mind and break the knee-jerk response to do something harmful.
- **Use a mood tracker:** Write down the day's events and your mood level. If you notice a consistent drop in mood at a certain time, you can prepare healthy coping actions.

Self-awareness is a skill that improves with practice. Over time, you learn to spot signs of internal tension before you act out a harmful habit. This can lead to better self-control and more confidence in your day-to-day decisions.

13. One Step at a Time: Avoid Overload

It might be tempting to try to fix all harmful habits at once. However, taking on too many changes can lead to feeling overwhelmed, which can cause you to abandon all your efforts. Instead, pick one or two key habits to address first.

- **Prioritize:** Which habit is causing the biggest damage right now? Start there. It could be substance use, anger issues, or procrastination.
- **Track small wins:** Each week, look back and see what went right, not just what went wrong. Reward yourself for small victories.
- **Stay realistic:** Change often takes longer than we expect. Be patient. Trying to force a major change in a few days usually ends in frustration.

Once you gain control over the top issues, move on to the next ones. This staged approach avoids overload and helps each new behavior become more solid before you tackle another challenge.

14. Getting Professional Help for Habit Change

Some habits are so strong or tied to deeper issues that a man might not be able to break them alone. In these cases, professional help from a counselor, therapist, or doctor can make a big difference. These experts can provide strategies tailored to your situation.

- **Therapy approaches:** Methods like cognitive behavioral therapy can help you spot negative thought patterns that drive harmful habits. A therapist can teach you ways to replace those thoughts with healthier ones.
- **Support groups:** For addictions (like alcohol or gambling), support groups can offer a community of people with similar experiences. This reduces shame and provides accountability.
- **Medication:** In some cases, a doctor might prescribe medication to handle severe anxiety or depression that fuels harmful habits. This is not a "magic fix," but it can help level mood so that other changes are easier to maintain.

Asking for professional help is not a sign of weakness. It is a practical decision to bring in more tools when you are working on an important goal.

---

15. The Value of Setting Firm Routines

Men who feel depressed may find it hard to keep structure in their days. A lack of structure can make it easier to fall into harmful habits. A clear routine can reduce guesswork and lower temptation to slip back into negative patterns.

- **Wake-up time and bedtime:** Keeping these mostly the same each day supports better sleep. Good sleep helps with mood regulation.
- **Regular meal times:** Planning simple, balanced meals at set times can help avoid random eating of junk food.
- **Exercise blocks:** Even short walks or workouts can be scheduled. When exercise is planned, you are more likely to follow through, creating a natural mood boost.
- **Work/relax balance:** If you schedule focused work periods and breaks, you reduce the risk of working until you burn out or procrastinating until it causes more stress.

A man does not need a rigid schedule, but having a broad plan for each day can keep him on track. It also helps break the cycle of random decisions that often lead to bad habits.

16. Checking the Deeper Reasons

Sometimes harmful habits are a cover for deeper emotional wounds or fears. If a man finds it extremely hard to stop a habit, he might ask if there is an underlying pain or unresolved issue. For example, he might be trying to forget a past trauma, worry about abandonment, or fear failure in a relationship.

- **Journaling sessions:** Write a paragraph each day about what is on your mind. Over time, patterns might appear about unresolved issues driving your actions.
- **Talking to a counselor:** A professional can help uncover hidden problems you may not see on your own.
- **Reflecting on triggers:** Notice if certain events or memories make you want to return to the habit. This could be a clue about deeper pain.

Addressing the root cause can create lasting change. Men often find that once they handle the emotional wound, the destructive habit loses its grip.

17. Chapter Summary

Breaking harmful habits is not just about quitting a single behavior. It involves understanding why the habit formed, recognizing triggers, and replacing it with better actions that meet real needs. A man might need to set boundaries, change parts of his daily routine, and seek help from friends, family, or professionals.

It is also important to be patient and kind to yourself during the process. Slip-ups will happen. The key is to learn from them, rather than letting them derail your efforts. With each successful step, self-esteem grows. Over time, replacing harmful habits with positive ones can lift mood, protect health, and improve relationships.

In the next chapter, we will move forward to **helpful tools for the mind**. We will talk about practical methods men can use to strengthen their mental state. These will include simple practices that can fit into a busy life without much extra cost or time. By adding the right mental habits, men can manage sadness more effectively and maintain long-term improvement.

CHAPTER 6: HELPFUL TOOLS FOR THE MIND

Men facing sadness or stress can benefit from practical tools that boost mental clarity and resilience. While formal therapy is one approach, there are also day-to-day exercises and methods that can make a big difference. In this chapter, we will explore a range of helpful tools that are easy to start using and do not require expensive resources. Many can be done at home, on a lunch break, or even while commuting.

These methods are backed by mental health experts, but they do not replace professional care if severe depression is present. Rather, they serve as strong support for men who want to feel more balanced in their thoughts and emotions. From simple breathing drills to journaling ideas, these tools can help men take greater control of their mental well-being.

---

1. Mindful Breathing

One of the simplest and most accessible tools is mindful breathing. This involves paying attention to each breath as it goes in and out of the body. It might sound too basic at first, but it has proven effects on reducing stress and helping clear a busy mind.

- **How to do it:** Sit or stand comfortably, close your eyes if you want, and take slow, steady breaths through the nose. Focus on the sensation of air moving in and out. If your mind wanders, gently bring it back to the breathing.
- **When to use it:** Try it for a couple of minutes in the morning or during a break. It can also be helpful right before a stressful event, such as a difficult meeting.
- **Benefits:** Lowers heart rate, eases muscle tension, and gives the mind a calm point of focus.

If you practice mindful breathing each day, you might notice you feel calmer and more in control of your thoughts. This simple act can reduce the intensity of racing thoughts that come with sadness or worry.

---

2. Journaling

Writing down thoughts can help sort through worries and spot patterns. Men sometimes avoid writing about feelings because it may seem odd at first. However, a short daily journal can give men a private space to let out tension.

- **Free writing:** Pick a set time each day—maybe before bed—and write nonstop for five minutes. Do not worry about grammar or structure. Let the words flow about anything on your mind.
- **Prompt-based journaling:** You can use prompts like, "Today I felt good about..." or "I'm worried about..." This provides a structure to guide your writing.
- **Tracking progress:** You might note triggers that made you feel down, as well as moments that lifted your spirits. Over time, you will see patterns and learn what boosts or lowers your mood.

Journaling can be kept secret if you want. The benefit is in the process of seeing your thoughts laid out clearly. It often leads to small insights: "I feel low when I skip breakfast" or "I get edgy after talking to this person." Recognizing these patterns helps you make smarter choices.

---

3. Physical Exercise

Exercise is not just for building muscles or losing weight. It can also support a healthier mind. When you move your body, certain chemicals (like endorphins) are released. These chemicals can improve mood and reduce stress. Regular exercise can also increase confidence over time.

- **Types of exercise:** There is no single best way to move. You could do short walks, jog, lift weights, or do home workouts with basic equipment. Even light stretching can help if done regularly.
- **Frequency:** Aiming for around 30 minutes of moderate movement most days can yield benefits. Start small if you are not used to exercise. Even 10-minute sessions count.
- **Social aspect:** Some men prefer working out alone, while others enjoy group sports or gym classes. Both are fine. Choose an approach that you can stick with.

If exercise is new to you, check with a doctor before starting, especially if you have health concerns. Small steps, such as taking the stairs or walking around the block, can build a foundation. Over time, you might enjoy the routine and notice improved mood and energy.

---

4. Positive Affirmations

Our thoughts guide our feelings more than we realize. If we keep telling ourselves we are not good enough, our mind will follow that track. Positive affirmations are short, uplifting statements you repeat to yourself to foster a better mindset.

- **Examples:** "I can handle today's challenges." "I am learning and growing each day." "My worth is not defined by my mistakes."
- **When to say them:** Some men say these affirmations in the morning to set a positive tone. Others repeat them before stressful tasks. You can even write them on sticky notes and place them where you will see them.
- **Why they help:** By replacing negative self-talk with more balanced statements, you gradually reshape your thinking. Repeated statements can rewire the brain's tendency to jump to negative ideas.

Some men find it odd to speak well of themselves, especially if they are used to self-criticism. But with regular practice, affirmations can become a quick tool to push back against the wave of negative thoughts.

---

5. Goal-Setting Techniques

Setting goals gives structure and motivation. Men dealing with sadness might feel directionless, as if each day blends into the next. Having specific targets can bring focus and a sense of purpose.

- **SMART goals:** This popular format stands for Specific, Measurable, Achievable, Relevant, and Time-bound. For instance, "I will walk for 20 minutes, three times a week, for the next month."
- **Short-term vs. long-term:** Combine small weekly goals with bigger plans for the next few months. Short-term goals give quick wins, and long-term goals provide a vision for the future.
- **Tracking and rewards:** Use a basic chart or app to mark progress. Celebrate small wins with a treat that does not cause more harm, like watching a favorite movie or enjoying a healthy snack.

Goal-setting can be done in many areas: fitness, work tasks, social connections, or personal skills. Watching progress can build confidence, which is often lacking when a man is feeling low.

---

6. Relaxation Exercises

Stress can make depression symptoms worse. Learning simple relaxation exercises can help. These can be done almost anywhere and do not require special gear.

- **Progressive muscle relaxation:** Start at your toes, tense the muscles for a few seconds, then release. Move up to the calves, thighs, and so on, all the way to your face. This teaches your body the difference between tension and relaxation.
- **Visualization:** Close your eyes and picture a peaceful scene, such as a calm lake or a quiet forest path. Focus on the details—what you see, hear, and feel. This can slow racing thoughts.
- **Simple stretches:** Even light stretches of the neck, shoulders, and back can relieve physical tension. This is useful if you spend a lot of time sitting or if stress causes tightness in your muscles.

Regular use of relaxation exercises can lower stress hormones in the body, helping men feel more stable and less overwhelmed.

---

7. Social Interaction Skills

Men who feel sad often isolate themselves. Learning basic social interaction skills can help break that cycle. This does not require becoming an extreme extrovert. Even a small improvement can build positive connections.

- **Active listening:** Practice giving someone full attention when they speak. Ask follow-up questions rather than jumping in with your own story. People tend to respond well when they feel heard.
- **Finding common ground:** If you share a hobby or interest with someone, mention it as a point of connection. This can spark a friendly exchange and reduce awkwardness.
- **Open body language:** Keep your arms uncrossed and maintain comfortable eye contact. This makes you appear more approachable.

- **Seek safe groups:** Look for group activities that match your interests, such as book clubs or casual sports leagues. The shared focus can ease social anxiety.

Developing social skills does not mean forcing yourself into huge gatherings. It means being more present and interactive when you do choose to connect with others.

---

8. Healthy Sleep Practices

Good sleep is a cornerstone of mental health. Lack of sleep can worsen low mood and make it harder to think clearly. Men who have trouble sleeping might find that sadness and irritability rise the next day. Improving sleep can bring a noticeable lift to mood.

- **Set a sleep schedule:** Go to bed and wake up at the same time each day. Consistency helps the body's internal clock.
- **Create a calm bedtime routine:** Avoid screens and bright lights before sleep. Maybe read a light book or do a short meditation.
- **Limit caffeine and alcohol:** Stimulants or late-night drinks can disrupt sleep quality, even if they seem to help you relax at first.
- **Check your bedroom environment:** A cool, dark, and quiet room supports better rest.

Even small changes, like avoiding screens 30 minutes before bed, can have a big impact. Rest is not a luxury; it is necessary for emotional balance.

---

9. Balanced Nutrition

A balanced diet supports both body and mind. While food alone cannot cure sadness, certain nutrients can help maintain stable energy and mood. Men who skip meals or eat mostly fast food may experience more fatigue and irritability.

- **Steady eating schedule:** Try not to skip breakfast or go long hours without a small meal. A drop in blood sugar can worsen mood swings.
- **Include fruits and veggies:** Fresh produce provides vitamins and minerals that keep the brain functioning well.
- **Proteins and healthy fats:** Lean meats, beans, eggs, nuts, and avocados can help keep you fuller and more focused.

- **Stay hydrated:** Dehydration can make you feel more tired or stressed without realizing the reason.

You do not need a fancy or complex diet. Simple, balanced choices can support a better mental state, especially when combined with other tools.

10. Limiting Negative News and Media Overload

Constant exposure to depressing or frightening news can drag a person down. Men might watch news channels or scroll through feeds for hours, not realizing how it affects their mood. Being informed is good, but there is a difference between staying updated and overloading on negativity.

- **Set a time limit:** Decide on a reasonable amount of news or social media per day, such as 15–20 minutes. Stick to it.
- **Choose quality sources:** Seek balanced news outlets rather than those that spin stories in alarming ways.
- **Filter content:** Some platforms allow you to mute or hide posts and accounts that cause unnecessary stress.
- **Check emotional state:** Notice how you feel after reading certain news stories. If they leave you anxious or hopeless, consider cutting back.

Reducing negativity in your media diet can help you feel less burdened, giving you more mental energy to address real life challenges.

11. Using Apps and Online Tools

Technology can be helpful for managing mental health. Many apps and websites offer guided exercises, trackers, and community support. This can be a good solution for men who do not want to attend formal programs right away.

- **Meditation apps:** Some apps walk you through breathing exercises or guided calm sessions. Many have beginner-friendly options.
- **Mood tracking apps:** These allow you to log your mood daily and note any triggers or events that might have caused changes.
- **Online support communities:** Some forums or groups focus on men's mental health. They offer a place to share stories, ask questions, and get tips from peers.

Take some time to read reviews and pick tools that fit your style. If something feels overwhelming or unhelpful, try a different approach. The goal is to have an easy way to watch your progress and get ideas for coping.

12. Self-Compassion Exercises

Men often judge themselves harshly. When sadness hits, they might feel like they are not measuring up to an internal standard. Self-compassion is the practice of treating yourself with kindness instead of constant self-criticism.

- **Speak to yourself as you would a friend:** If a friend was going through a hard time, you would probably say supportive things. Apply the same kindness to yourself.
- **Acknowledge feelings:** It is okay to feel low sometimes. Telling yourself, "This is hard, and it's normal to feel upset" can reduce shame.
- **Short meditations on kindness:** Spend a minute focusing on a phrase like, "May I learn to be kind to myself." This might sound unusual at first, but it can soften harsh self-talk.

Being kind to yourself does not mean avoiding responsibility. It means recognizing that you are human and allowed to struggle without tearing yourself down in the process.

13. Relaxing Hobbies

Hobbies are not just for passing time; they can help restore energy and excitement. Engaging in something enjoyable can break up the gloom that comes with persistent sadness.

- **Examples of hobbies:** Gardening, painting, cooking, playing an instrument, mild sports, or any creative project.
- **Group vs. solo:** Choose an activity you can do alone if you need quiet time, or find a group-based hobby if you want social interaction. Both can help your mind in different ways.
- **Balance:** Make sure the hobby does not become another area of stress if you start to push yourself too hard. Keep it casual and fun.

Having even 30 minutes a few times a week for a hobby can be a mood booster and distract from negative thoughts.

14. Gratitude Practice

Focusing on what is going right can help counterbalance the brain's habit of focusing on problems. A gratitude practice does not ignore troubles; it just helps you notice the good things that still exist around you.

- **Daily list:** Write down 3 things you are thankful for each day. These can be small, like enjoying a hot cup of tea or finishing a project.
- **Thank-you notes:** Show appreciation to someone who helped you. This can be a quick text, an email, or a short face-to-face thank you.
- **Gratitude moments:** Pause during the day to notice nice weather, a kind gesture, or something you like about yourself.

This shift in perspective can create a slight boost in mood. It also makes it easier to see that not everything is negative, even when life is hard.

15. Setting Up a Support System

A strong support system does not have to be large. It just needs to consist of people, groups, or professionals you trust and can reach out to when you feel down.

- **Friends and family:** Even one close friend who truly listens can make a difference.
- **Online or local groups:** These can include support circles or men's clubs. They provide a space to share experiences.
- **Professionals:** A counselor, doctor, or mental health hotline can be part of your safety network. Save important numbers in your phone for easy access.
- **Emergency plan:** If you ever feel overwhelmed, have a plan in place. This might include calling a trusted person or going to a walk-in clinic. Planning ahead can ease panic if crisis hits.

You do not have to share everything with everyone. The idea is to have different sources of help for different needs. Some men prefer professional help for deep issues and casual friends for everyday chatting.

16. Checking Progress Regularly

Using these tools is not a one-time event. It is helpful to check in every week or month to see what is working and what is not. This keeps you from drifting back into old patterns without noticing.

- **Weekly review:** Pick a day to look back at how often you used a tool. Did it help? If not, why?
- **Adjust as needed:** If a certain exercise or plan no longer works, do not force it. Try a new one or tweak the old approach.
- **Celebrate small wins:** Mark down improvements, such as sleeping better, feeling less anger, or getting tasks done on time.

Men who actively check their progress tend to stick with helpful routines. It also prevents losing momentum during busy or stressful times.

17. Chapter Summary

Mental tools can support men who are dealing with sadness or stress. Methods like mindful breathing, journaling, and regular exercise can ease tension and bring fresh energy. Positive affirmations, goal-setting, and relaxation exercises all help shape a calmer mindset. By working on social skills, sleep habits, and healthy eating, men can strengthen their mental foundation.

There are many ways to personalize these tools. Not every idea fits every man's style or schedule. Trying a few at a time and noting which ones give the best results can lead to a stronger overall approach. In the chapters to come, we will look deeper into reaching out for help, maintaining physical health, and managing issues like work stress and family demands. Each new piece of knowledge can add to your collection of resources, giving you more confidence in handling the ups and downs of life.

Remember, using helpful tools is a sign of self-care and wisdom. You do not need to be in crisis to benefit from them. In fact, men who use these simple methods regularly often report feeling more balanced, less isolated, and better prepared for life's challenges.

CHAPTER 7: HOW TO REACH OUT FOR HELP

Reaching out for help is a turning point for many men who feel low or overwhelmed. Yet, some hold back because they worry about being judged, or they believe they should solve their problems on their own. This chapter will offer clear guidance on how to ask for help in different ways. It will explain why asking for help can make a positive difference, and it will give tips on what to say and whom to trust. By reading these sections, men can see that there are many types of support, both formal and informal. They will also learn how to handle any setbacks they might face when first trying to speak up.

We will look at problems that block men from asking for help, such as feeling weak or fearing what others might think. We will share ideas on how to get support from family, friends, professionals, and community resources. We will also mention practical steps a man can take if he feels he is not getting the support he needs. By the end of this chapter, the idea of reaching out may seem less intimidating, and readers can feel more prepared to take that first brave step.

---

1. Why Asking for Help Matters

Asking for help is not a sign of failure. It is a practical solution when sadness or stress reaches a level that interferes with normal life. Men sometimes hold the view that they must handle everything alone, but this can lead to isolation and worse moods. When we share a concern or worry with the right person, it often feels like a burden has eased.

In many situations, a friend or professional may notice an issue that is not obvious to us. They can suggest ideas or point out resources we never knew existed. Asking for help also reminds us that we do not have to carry heavy loads on our own. Knowing that someone is there to listen can bring a sense of relief. It may also be a step toward proper care, such as therapy or support groups. In short, asking for help matters because it shows we value our well-being and deserve guidance when things feel too hard.

---

2. Common Barriers That Stop Men from Seeking Help

Men face many internal and external barriers that keep them silent. One big barrier is the fear of appearing weak. Another is the belief that real men should solve problems alone. These ideas can keep men stuck in low moods for longer than needed. Some men worry that reaching out might damage their reputation at work or among friends.

There might also be a feeling of shame. A man might think, "I should be able to handle this without help." On top of that, cultural messages can discourage men from sharing personal struggles. Media often highlights tough male figures who never talk about fear or sadness. That can form an unrealistic image of what a man should look like. As a result, men might doubt whether their issues are serious enough to ask for help. Recognizing these barriers is the first step to breaking them.

---

3. When to Consider Outside Support

It can be hard for men to decide when it is time to seek help. Some assume that if they can still go to work, pay bills, or smile sometimes, they are not "bad enough" to need support. However, any ongoing sadness, worry, or behavior change that disrupts life is a clue that outside support might help. For instance, if a man notices his moods are affecting relationships at home or his ability to concentrate at work, it might be a sign to talk to someone.

Sleep problems or repeated thoughts of quitting important tasks are also signals that professional guidance could be helpful. It is wise not to wait for a complete crisis. The earlier men talk to a friend, counselor, or doctor, the easier it can be to prevent more serious concerns. Outside support does not always mean formal therapy right away; it can start with a trusted person who listens without judging.

---

4. The Role of Friends and Family

Friends and family members can be the first line of help. They know the man's history, personality, and the details of his life. Sometimes, just telling a loved one about feeling low can provide a sense of relief. Support from close people can look like regular check-ins by phone, short visits, or even going for walks together. Having someone who cares can lessen the feeling of being alone.

Family members can also encourage men to take the next step if needed, like seeing a doctor or counselor. They might point out changes in behavior that the man himself has not noticed. They can also offer practical support, like helping with errands or giving a place to rest if stress at home is high. Not every man has supportive family and friends, but those who do can benefit greatly by opening up to them when times are tough.

---

5. Speaking with a Professional

Professional help involves talking to someone trained in mental health, such as a counselor, therapist, or psychologist. These experts have studied human emotions, thought patterns, and methods to guide clients toward healthier habits. They do not usually focus on judging or labeling; instead, they aim to give strategies for improvement.

One advantage of speaking with a professional is privacy. Therapists are bound by confidentiality rules, which makes it easier to share personal thoughts. Another plus is that a professional approach is structured and goal-oriented. Men can learn new coping skills, gain insight into their sadness, and develop a plan to handle stress or harmful thoughts. Appointments can vary in number; some people benefit from short-term counseling, while others stick with regular sessions for a longer period.

---

6. What to Expect in Therapy

Many men feel anxious about what will happen in a therapy session. It might help to know that the first session usually involves discussing why you came and what you hope to gain. The therapist may ask questions about your background, current stressors, and general well-being. This is not meant to pry but to form a complete picture of your situation.

Therapy then moves at a pace that feels comfortable. You might talk about daily challenges, past experiences, or fears for the future. A good therapist should guide the conversation in a supportive manner and may suggest homework exercises—simple tasks to practice new habits. Sessions can last around 45 to 60 minutes. Over time, therapy can help men see patterns in their thoughts and behaviors, then learn tools to adjust unhelpful patterns. While it may feel awkward at first, many men find relief in having a confidential space to open up.

7. Different Kinds of Therapy

Not all therapy styles are the same. Some counselors use a method known as cognitive behavioral therapy (CBT). This type focuses on how thoughts affect feelings. It offers ways to spot unhelpful thought patterns and replace them with more balanced ones. Another style is psychodynamic therapy, which looks at how past events shape current behavior. There is also interpersonal therapy, which deals with relationship skills and resolving conflicts.

Men might also find group therapy helpful. In a group setting, participants share experiences under a therapist's supervision. This allows men to see they are not alone in their struggles, which can be comforting. Some groups also teach practical skills for anger control, stress management, or social interaction. Reading about these different approaches can help men pick a therapy style that best fits their personality and goals.

8. Online Help Options

In recent years, online mental health resources have grown. Men who feel uneasy about face-to-face sessions can try online therapy platforms. These services connect clients with licensed therapists through video calls, voice calls, or chat messages. It can be done from the comfort of home, which removes barriers like travel time or the fear of being seen going to a therapist's office.

Other online options include text hotlines, mental health forums, and apps that teach coping strategies or mood tracking. Some men prefer digital support because it feels more private, and they can access it at flexible times. While online support might not replace in-person treatment for serious cases, it can still be an effective choice for many people. It also offers the chance to seek help quickly, without waiting for a face-to-face appointment.

9. Finding the Right Therapist or Counselor

Choosing the right therapist is important. A good fit can make a big difference in how comfortable a man feels speaking openly. Consider factors such as the therapist's background, style, and area of specialization. Some specialize in male mental health, trauma, or addiction issues. If you have health insurance, check which providers are covered. You can also read online reviews or ask friends if they recommend someone.

Do not feel bad if the first therapist you meet is not the right match. It is common to try a few before finding one who suits your communication style and goals. Therapists themselves know how crucial the right fit is, so they do not usually take offense if you decide to look elsewhere. The aim is to find someone who listens well, provides constructive feedback, and helps you feel at ease.

---

10. Using Hotlines and Crisis Services

If a man feels he might harm himself or is overwhelmed with thoughts that he cannot manage, a hotline or crisis service can be a lifesaver. Hotlines are staffed by people who are trained to handle urgent emotional distress. You can call and speak anonymously, which can help if you are not ready to see a therapist in person. They offer a listening ear and can guide you to local resources.

Some hotlines focus on specific problems, such as substance issues, suicidal thoughts, or domestic conflicts. If you are ever in immediate danger or risk, do not hesitate to call emergency services or go to a hospital. Crisis lines might also offer text or online chat. This can be helpful for men who do not like talking on the phone. Remember, calling a hotline does not mean you are weak; it means you are taking a responsible step to protect yourself.

---

11. Community Groups and Local Resources

Beyond professional therapy, community groups offer low-cost or free support. Look for local organizations, churches, or health centers that run support circles for men. These groups can be centered on specific topics, such as anger management, grief, or relationship issues. By attending regular meetings, men can share experiences, learn coping strategies, and build connections in a supportive setting.

Local resources might also include classes on stress relief or workshops led by mental health educators. These can give men a chance to practice skills in a structured environment. Community groups are a good option if cost is a concern, because many of them are funded by donations or grants. The sense of belonging and understanding from people in similar life situations can help cut down on loneliness and shame.

---

12. Approaching Support at Work

Some workplaces offer mental health programs as part of employee benefits. Known as Employee Assistance Programs (EAPs), these can provide short-term counseling or referrals to outside providers. Men may hesitate to use EAPs, fearing coworkers or bosses might find out. However, these programs typically protect the user's privacy. No personal details are shared with managers unless there is a serious risk issue.

If an EAP is not available, a man can still speak privately with human resources to find out about any wellness programs or time-off options for mental health. Some companies allow flexible schedules or personal days to handle stress or attend therapy. Taking advantage of these offerings does not show weakness. It shows a commitment to staying healthy and productive. Using workplace support can also reduce the expense of therapy if it is partially covered.

---

13. What to Say When Reaching Out

Starting the conversation can be the hardest part. A man might worry about how to explain his feelings or fear he will not find the right words. Simpler is often better. You can start with "I've been feeling really low lately and I'm not sure what to do," or "I'm going through something hard right now, and I need someone to talk to."

If you are speaking to a professional, you can say something like, "I have been feeling sad for a few months, and it's affecting my sleep and focus. I'd like to learn how to manage it." In a group setting, you might introduce yourself and mention a short version of what brought you there. People do not expect a perfect script; honesty goes a long way. Saying even a few words of truth can open the door to more detailed discussions over time.

14. Helping Someone Else Seek Help

Sometimes you might be the one who sees a friend, coworker, or family member struggling. Offering help can be tricky if the person is not ready to talk. One of the best approaches is to ask simple, genuine questions: "How have you been feeling?" or "Is something bothering you?" Let them speak without interruption. If they seem defensive, do not push too hard. Keep a calm and supportive tone.

You could mention resources, like a local counselor or a trusted online community, but avoid flooding them with solutions before they ask for them. If you worry they might harm themselves, you can share a hotline number or urge them to see a doctor. In an emergency, do not hesitate to call professional services. Being there for someone else can be a big help, but remember you are not responsible for fixing all of their problems. Encourage them to seek professional help when it goes beyond what a friend can do.

15. Handling Rejection or Unhelpful Responses

Not everyone responds kindly when a man opens up. A friend might dismiss the concerns or change the subject. A family member might say something insensitive. These reactions can be painful, but they do not mean your feelings are invalid. It might mean that person does not know how to respond or has their own fears about mental health.

Instead of giving up, understand that one poor response does not represent everyone. Try speaking to another friend or contacting a hotline. Men can also share with support groups or professionals who are trained to offer understanding. Keep in mind that your worth does not depend on one person's ability to respond well. People have different abilities and experiences. The important thing is to keep looking for the help you need, because it is out there.

16. Building a Personal Support Network

A solid support network is not formed overnight. It often starts with one or two trusted people—a best friend, sibling, or counselor. Over time, you might find a coworker who relates to your experiences or join a community group that focuses on mental wellness. By speaking with more people and forming genuine connections, you enlarge your support circle.

This network could also include online friends or mentors. The point is to have a mix of people you can lean on when life gets tough. Some might provide emotional comfort, while others might give practical tips or just a fun distraction. Letting people know you appreciate their help is good for both parties. It reinforces that the relationship is important and that being open is valuable.

---

17. Practical Steps to Start Asking for Help

To avoid feeling stuck, it helps to outline small steps. First, list one or two people you feel somewhat safe talking to. Plan a simple script in your head so you know what you want to say. Pick a calm moment—maybe after work or when you both have free time. Send a short text or make a brief phone call: "Hey, can we talk? I've been having a hard time."

If you prefer professional help, search online for local therapists or call your health insurance for a list of approved providers. Write down a few questions to ask the therapist on the phone, like, "Do you have experience working with men who feel depressed?" If cost is an issue, ask about sliding-scale fees or free community options. Taking these direct actions can break the habit of waiting and hoping things will fix themselves.

---

18. Chapter Summary

Reaching out for help is often a key step for men dealing with sadness. While fears about judgment or showing weakness can be strong, asking for support does not reduce a man's value. In fact, it can be a wise, responsible act that leads to new solutions. Friends and family might be the first to offer comfort, but professional help can also guide men toward deeper healing. If one approach does not work, there are many others, such as online tools, local groups, hotlines, or workplace programs.

CHAPTER 8: PHYSICAL HEALTH AND THE MIND

Physical and mental health are closely connected. When a man is run-down, not eating well, or skipping regular movement, it can worsen sadness and stress. On the other hand, simple actions like regular exercise, healthy meals, and proper rest can boost mood and energy. This chapter looks at how body health influences thoughts and emotions. We will give facts that might not always appear in casual discussions. We will also give tips on building strong body habits without extreme changes that are hard to keep.

Some men think caring for physical well-being is mostly about looking fit or lifting the heaviest weights at the gym. While fitness can be part of it, the link between mind and body goes deeper than looks. We will show how hormones, brain chemicals, and even gut health can affect how you feel day to day. By the end, readers will see that caring for the body is not a luxury but a key piece of managing low moods and anxiety.

---

1. Why Physical Health Affects Mental State

The body and mind share a strong link through nerves, hormones, and other chemicals. If the body is tired or stressed, the brain often reflects that strain. For example, when a man does not sleep enough, certain areas of the brain that regulate emotions may not function as well. This can cause mood swings or make negative thoughts more intense.

Blood sugar levels also affect mental clarity. Too many sugary foods can cause energy spikes and crashes, which then affect mood stability. Another important connection is through movement. When muscles move, the body releases endorphins. These are natural chemicals that help create a calmer or happier state. If a man's lifestyle lacks movement, the body might not produce enough of these helpful substances. All of these factors show that physical health is not just about strength or appearance. It is tied to mood regulation and clear thinking.

---

2. The Role of Nutrition

Nutrition is the foundation for many body processes. What we eat supplies vitamins, minerals, and energy that help the brain function. Certain nutrients, like omega-3 fatty acids found in fish or flaxseeds, support brain health. Deficiencies in vitamins such as vitamin D or B-complex can lead to fatigue, poor concentration, and even irritability.

Protein is another key element. It aids in building and repairing tissues, including brain cells. Lean sources like chicken, beans, or low-fat dairy can support mental alertness. Carbohydrates, especially those from whole grains, offer slow-release energy. This can help keep mood steady instead of causing sudden sugar spikes. Meanwhile, too many sweets or processed foods can increase inflammation in the body, and some research links chronic inflammation to higher rates of depression. While nutrition alone might not fix severe sadness, it can greatly influence a man's energy and emotional stability.

---

3. Hydration and Brain Function

Water intake can also shape how we feel. The human brain is mostly water. When we do not drink enough fluids, even mild dehydration can trigger headaches, dizziness, and mental fog. These issues make it harder to handle daily stress. A man who regularly forgets to drink water might notice lower concentration and more frequent frustration.

Thirst can sometimes mask itself as hunger or tiredness. If you find yourself irritable in the middle of the day, a glass of water might ease that feeling better than coffee or sugary drinks. Coffee, in moderate amounts, can boost alertness, but too much may raise anxiety. Balancing coffee intake with water is often wise, especially for men who notice shaky hands or racing thoughts after several cups. Keeping a water bottle nearby and taking sips throughout the day is an easy way to support steady mental function.

---

4. Hormones and Testosterone

Testosterone has a big impact on a man's physical and mental state. Low testosterone levels can lead to lower energy, reduced drive, and mood shifts. While some of these shifts are mild, they can add up if left unchecked. Stress hormones like cortisol also play a part. Chronic stress can push cortisol levels too high, affecting sleep and mood over time.

Men over 30 may experience a gradual dip in testosterone, which can be normal. However, big drops could suggest an underlying issue. Doctors can do a simple blood test to check levels. If levels are significantly low, treatment might involve addressing stress or making lifestyle changes like more exercise, better sleep, or in some cases, testosterone therapy. Before making any major changes, men should talk to a healthcare provider to avoid guesswork about hormone health.

5. Importance of Regular Movement

Exercise can lift mood in ways that go beyond fitness gains. When the body moves, it triggers the release of endorphins, which many people call "feel-good chemicals." These substances can ease stress and improve mental clarity. Even moderate exercise, like brisk walking or biking, can help. It does not require marathon training or heavy lifting to see results.

Consistency matters more than intensity. A man who walks 20 minutes each day may see more benefits than someone who does a single hard workout once a week. Moving in nature, such as hiking or jogging in a park, can reduce anxiety further by offering fresh air and sunlight. The sense of accomplishment from sticking to a routine can also boost confidence. If starting a new plan, it is best to begin gently and build up as strength and energy grow.

6. Sleep and Mental Balance

Getting enough quality rest is one of the best ways to support mood. During sleep, the body repairs tissues and organizes thoughts. If a man sleeps poorly, the next day can feel like an uphill battle. It becomes harder to concentrate, and little annoyances might turn into big irritations.

People vary in how much sleep they need, but most adults do best with about seven to nine hours per night. A consistent bedtime and wake-up time help regulate the internal clock. Good sleep hygiene includes avoiding heavy meals or bright screens before bed. If falling asleep is an issue, a bedtime routine—such as reading a relaxing book or doing gentle stretches—can calm the mind. A lack of proper sleep over many months can raise the risk of deeper sadness or anxiety. So, making sleep a priority is not optional. It is essential for mental health.

7. Managing Physical Stress

Physical stress can come from many areas: high-pressure jobs that require long hours, manual labor without proper breaks, or even caretaking roles for family members. When the body is pushed too hard, tension accumulates in muscles, often in the neck or shoulders. This can cause headaches or persistent aches. Over time, chronic muscle tension can feed negative moods because pain signals keep traveling to the brain.

Men can manage this stress by scheduling short rest periods, practicing gentle stretching, or trying a relaxation method like progressive muscle tensing and releasing. Some find that massage therapy reduces built-up tension. If a job is physically intense, using correct posture and taking regular water breaks can prevent exhaustion. Listening to what the body is telling you can be a lifesaver. Ignoring aches or fatigue might lead to bigger issues that harm both physical and mental well-being.

---

8. The Impact of Long Sitting Hours

Modern life often requires men to sit for long stretches at desks, in cars, or on couches. Long sitting periods reduce blood flow and can weaken certain muscles, like those in the core and lower back. Over time, this might lead to back pain or stiff joints, which then cause irritability.

Regularly standing or walking for a minute or two each hour can improve circulation. Doing light stretches at the desk can also help. If possible, switching to a standing desk for part of the day might reduce strain. When men are free from constant aches, they often find it easier to remain positive and focused. Small actions, like a five-minute walk during breaks, can stack up to offer mental benefits. It also gives the eyes a rest from staring at a screen, which can help with overall stress levels.

---

9. Balancing Work and Physical Activity

Finding time to be active can be tough if work hours are long or unpredictable. However, building small exercise sessions into the day can still make a difference. For instance, a man might park his car a bit farther from the office or use the stairs instead of the elevator. He could take a short walk after lunch. If evenings are hectic, setting aside just 15 or 20 minutes can be enough to break a sweat and release tension.

Some workplaces have onsite gyms or offer gym membership discounts. Taking advantage of these perks can be a good idea. A quick workout before heading home can help transition from a work mindset to personal time. If the job involves lots of physical labor, then the exercise goal might be more about gentle stretching or yoga to soothe sore muscles. The main point is to find a balance that supports both the job and physical health.

10. Outdoor Activities and Sunlight

Sunlight plays a big role in regulating the body's internal clock and mood. Not getting enough sunlight can lead to low vitamin D levels, which may contribute to fatigue or sadness. Spending time outdoors, even if it is just a 10-minute walk during a break, can help. Fresh air and natural scenery can also reduce mental fatigue.

Men who live in areas with long, dark winters sometimes experience low mood or a condition known as seasonal sadness. A special light therapy box can help replace natural sunlight during those months. Outdoor activities like light gardening, cycling, or walking the dog can serve a dual purpose of exercise and sunlight exposure. Regularly stepping outside is an easy way to boost mental health, especially when combined with moderate physical movement.

11. Mind-Body Practices

Certain activities combine gentle movement with focused breathing. Examples include tai chi, yoga, and simple stretching routines. These practices can lower heart rate, reduce muscle tension, and calm anxious thoughts. They are often recommended for men who want a low-impact way to boost both physical and mental health.

These mind-body practices can be adapted to different fitness levels. Some men start with basic stretches or chair yoga if they have limited mobility. Others might join a beginner's class. The idea is to pay attention to each movement, which helps the mind avoid dwelling on worries. Over time, these techniques can train the nervous system to respond more calmly to stress. Many men find they become more patient in daily life after regularly practicing a mind-body exercise.

12. Building a Healthy Routine

Routines can keep life organized when the mind feels scattered. A well-rounded routine might include regular meal times, set periods for movement, and stable sleep schedules. Each part supports the others. For example, exercising in the late afternoon can improve the chance of sleeping better at night. Getting good rest then makes it easier to wake up for breakfast, which in turn helps maintain steady energy throughout the day.

A healthy routine does not have to be overly strict. The goal is to create a framework that supports consistent choices. Tracking progress in a simple notebook or on a phone can help. Men might record what they ate, how many hours they slept, or how they felt after exercising. Over time, patterns emerge, showing what boosts mood and what triggers low feelings. Adjusting the routine based on these insights can lead to lasting improvements.

13. Reducing Toxic Substances

Substances like alcohol, tobacco, or drugs can harm both body and mind if used often. Many men turn to these as coping methods for sadness or stress. While they might bring a brief sense of relief, the negative effects often outweigh any short-lived comfort. Alcohol, for example, can disrupt sleep cycles, leading to more tired mornings. Tobacco raises heart rate and blood pressure, and it can reduce lung capacity needed for physical activity.

Men who suspect they use these substances too frequently should consider speaking with a healthcare professional about safer ways to reduce or quit. Some workplaces offer programs to help employees quit smoking or cut back on drinking. Community centers and online groups also support men going through these changes. Cutting down on toxic substances can free the body to heal, which in turn can help improve mood and clear thinking.

14. The Gut-Brain Connection

One lesser-known area is the link between gut health and mental health. The gut has trillions of bacteria that help break down food and produce important chemicals. Some of these chemicals communicate with the brain and can influence mood. When the balance of gut bacteria is off, it can contribute to inflammation or other issues that might affect mental well-being.

Men can support gut health by eating foods rich in fiber, such as vegetables, fruits, and whole grains. Yogurt with live cultures or fermented foods like kimchi or sauerkraut can also encourage a healthy gut balance. Taking antibiotics or eating lots of sugary foods can upset the balance, so moderation is wise. While this might not be a cure for sadness, maintaining a healthy gut can be one piece of the puzzle in feeling better overall.

---

15. Sports and Team Activities

Group sports or classes add a social element to physical health. Men who feel lonely can benefit from meeting others while playing a sport or doing a group fitness activity. This can foster friendships, provide motivation to stay active, and give a sense of belonging. Even a casual pick-up basketball game or a walking club can bring these positive effects.

Team-based exercise can also push men to stay consistent. If you know your group is counting on you, you might be less likely to skip a session. Shared achievements, like improving at a sport or finishing a group goal, can improve self-esteem. Some men prefer more individual activities, which is fine, but those who are open to group interaction may find it doubles as social support and exercise.

---

16. Staying Aware of Physical Warning Signs

Men sometimes ignore physical signals like frequent headaches, constant fatigue, or unexplained aches. They might write them off as normal aging or just stress. However, these signals can be important. They could point to serious medical issues or they could be signs that the body is over-stressed. Paying attention allows a man to catch problems early.

If problems persist, a doctor's checkup might be in order. Routine tests can reveal if a man has certain deficiencies, like low iron or vitamin levels. A doctor might also spot early signs of conditions such as high blood pressure or diabetes, which can have mental health effects. Addressing these physical health issues often helps clear up mood concerns. It is better to be cautious and get answers than to endure problems that could be handled with early care.

17. Small, Consistent Changes

Big leaps can be exciting, but they can also cause burnout if they are too drastic. Instead of making extreme changes, many experts suggest small steps that can be maintained long term. For instance, a man might start by taking a 10-minute walk each evening instead of suddenly trying to run several miles. He might swap one sugary snack for a piece of fruit each day. Gradual changes are more likely to become permanent habits.

Over weeks and months, these small steps add up. A man could notice improved strength, better sleep, and a more stable mood. It is also easier to handle setbacks. If a busy week makes it hard to keep up with all changes, sticking to a few small ones is still possible. Over time, these modest improvements can build a solid base of physical health, which then supports a healthier mental state.

18. Chapter Summary

Physical health and mental health are deeply linked. A man who takes care of his body often finds that his mind feels clearer and more stable. This does not require extreme fitness programs or crash diets. Rather, it involves consistent, balanced habits like regular exercise, quality sleep, good nutrition, and managing stress. Paying attention to hormones, hydration, and the gut can also help.

In this chapter, we looked at how poor sleep, lack of movement, and unbalanced meals can worsen a man's low mood. We also covered how small daily actions, from standing more at work to eating fiber-rich foods, can support better mental well-being. No single trick fixes everything, but a combination of good body care and awareness can make a real difference. The next chapters will show further strategies for handling work pressure, family stress, and life's other demands. With a solid base in physical health, men have a stronger chance of keeping sadness at bay and finding a path toward feeling better.

CHAPTER 9: WORK, STRESS, AND FEELING LOW

Work can be a major source of pride and purpose. But it can also create a high level of stress. Many men feel pressure to provide, to meet deadlines, and to never show any sign of slowing down. Over time, these demands can build up, leading to low mood or even a deep sadness. This chapter will explore how work stress can affect a man's well-being, why some workplaces make stress worse, and how to deal with these challenges in practical ways. We will also point to some less common facts about job-related stress that might not be widely known. By the end, the goal is to show that managing work pressure can be done step by step, without giving up on a career or sense of responsibility.

---

1. Why Work Stress Hits So Hard

Work stress can drain a man's mental and physical energy because it often follows him outside of working hours. A person might clock out, but lingering thoughts about emails, problems, or upcoming tasks can keep churning in his mind. This ongoing mental load can upset sleep patterns, reduce patience at home, and sap enjoyment from free time. Over the weeks and months, that adds up.

Key points to note about why work stress is unique:

- **Constant performance demands:** Many jobs require consistent output. Men can feel judged if they have a single off day.
- **Financial worries:** Stress is higher if a man feels his job is the main source of family income. Losing it could mean financial trouble.
- **Limited recovery time:** Some men have long commutes, or they bring work home. This lowers the chance to rest and recharge.

In many work settings, men are expected to appear confident at all times. This can make it hard to admit when stress is overwhelming. That is why men who face pressure at work may try to hide it until it becomes unbearable.

---

2. Hidden Traps in Modern Work Environments

Modern offices and job sites may have features that unknowingly increase stress:

- **Open office plans** with no privacy can lead to constant noise and interruptions. This makes it hard to focus and raises anxiety.
- **Always-on communication** via email or phone can blur the line between work and home. A man might feel he can never fully switch off.
- **Tight deadlines** or frequent "urgent" tasks can keep adrenaline high. While a bit of adrenaline can help performance, too much for too long leads to fatigue.
- **Insecure job markets** cause men to fear layoffs. They might work extra hours to appear dedicated, even if it hurts health.

Less recognized is how small daily hassles, like computer slow-downs or a lack of clear instructions, can pile up. Each small frustration on its own might not be huge, but together they build a tense environment. Over time, tension can become the default state.

---

3. Signs Work Stress Is Leading to Low Mood

A man might not always connect his sadness to work. He might just think he is tired or cranky. But here are clues that job pressure may be a root cause:

1. **Dreading work on Sunday night:** A strong sense of doom as the weekend ends can signal that the job atmosphere is toxic.
2. **Physical symptoms before or during work:** Headaches, stomach upset, or muscle tension that appear mainly on workdays.
3. **Irritability toward coworkers or customers:** Lashing out or snapping at small issues can be a sign of deeper frustration.
4. **Thinking about quitting constantly:** Frequent thoughts of walking out can mean the stress has crossed a healthy boundary.
5. **Feelings of failure or shame:** If a man believes he is not meeting expectations, he might feel worthless. This can darken his mood day after day.

These symptoms can affect performance. If a man is too anxious or sad to concentrate, his output may suffer, which could fuel more stress. It becomes a cycle that can be hard to break without direct action.

---

4. The Less Talked-About Effects on Life Outside Work

When stress from a job remains high, it can spill over into personal areas:

- **Sleep disruption:** A man might lie awake replaying work conflicts. Or he might have nightmares about missed deadlines or angry bosses.
- **Strain on relationships:** A short temper can lead to arguments at home. Loved ones may feel ignored if he is always preoccupied with work problems.
- **Social withdrawal:** A man might skip social events because he is too drained or worried about upcoming tasks. Over time, isolation can worsen sadness.
- **Unhealthy coping:** Some men might drink more alcohol after a hard day. Others might gamble, binge-watch shows all evening, or overeat to distract themselves from worries.

One hidden effect is the feeling of losing personal identity. A man might start to see himself only as a worker with no time for hobbies or friendships. This narrow focus can fuel feelings of emptiness if things go wrong at work. Recognizing these hidden effects can help men see the broader damage that excessive job stress can cause.

---

5. Golden Tips for Handling Work Stress

Below are a few practical, lesser-known strategies that can help manage job pressure:

1. **Micro-breaks:** Research shows that taking short, frequent pauses can reduce burnout. For example, every hour or so, stand up for 1–2 minutes, stretch, or look away from the screen. It sounds too simple, but these tiny resets help the brain recharge.
2. **Task batching:** Group similar tasks together. For instance, handle all email replies at set times rather than checking every few minutes. Constant interruptions can raise stress hormones in the body.
3. **Controlled technology use:** If possible, turn off work emails or notifications after certain hours. This gives the mind a clear boundary that work time is over.
4. **Positive self-acknowledgment:** Each day, note one thing that went well at work, even if it is small. This helps counter the negative pattern of only seeing failures or what went wrong.

5. **Active decompression after work:** Instead of going straight from the job to a stressful home environment, use a brief routine to relax. This could be a 5-minute walk, some calming music in the car, or even a quick breathing exercise before stepping into the house.

These tips might sound simple, but many men never try them or do them regularly. The key is consistency. Building a habit of small stress-managing actions can add up over time.

---

6. Communicating With Colleagues and Bosses

Talking about stress at work does not mean giving a dramatic speech. It can be done in calm, fact-based ways that address the workload or environment. Here are steps to consider:

- **Schedule a private chat:** Instead of complaining in the hallway, request a quiet moment to discuss concerns. This shows respect and seriousness.
- **Use concrete examples:** Rather than saying, "I'm so stressed," mention specific tasks or deadlines that seem impossible. Propose ideas, like adjusting priorities or asking for more time.
- **Suggest solutions:** Bosses often respond well if you come with possible fixes. For instance, "Could we move the team meeting so I have time to finish the monthly report without rushing?"
- **Stay professional:** Avoid blaming coworkers or using emotional language. Stick to the facts: "I've noticed that daily urgent tasks pull me away from my main projects, and my performance is slipping."

If the workplace is healthy, a manager might be open to adjusting workloads or offering flexible schedules. Some companies also have Employee Assistance Programs. These can provide counseling or training on stress management. Sadly, not all bosses are understanding. In that case, a man might have to decide if staying is worth the long-term harm to his well-being.

---

7. When It Might Be Time to Consider a Job Change

No job is perfect, and every position has stress. But sometimes the environment or demands are so toxic that a man cannot avoid harm unless he leaves. Signs it might be time to explore other options:

1. **Constant dread:** If every morning starts with a sense of panic or hopelessness, and efforts to fix the situation have failed, it might be time to move on.
2. **Health decline:** When stress causes major health problems, like frequent chest pains or severe insomnia, the cost might be too high.
3. **No path forward:** Some workplaces do not allow any negotiation or improvement in conditions. If you have tried and see no possible change, staying could lead to deeper sadness.
4. **Ethical conflicts:** If the job requires actions or behavior that clash with personal values, the mental strain can be immense.

Making a big change can be scary, especially if it affects finances. Planning a careful exit is often best. That might involve saving money, looking for new positions quietly, or gaining new skills to expand job options. Even though it is a major decision, escaping a harmful work environment can sometimes be the best step for long-term health.

---

8. Balancing Ambition with Well-Being

Men often feel pressured to climb the career ladder fast, to earn more, or to prove themselves. Ambition itself is not bad—it can lead to positive growth. But when ambition takes over every part of life, a man can neglect rest, relationships, and personal interests.

Ways to find balance:

- **Define success for yourself:** Ask what truly matters. Is it only about a job title and salary, or does success also mean a stable family life, free time, or good health?
- **Set boundaries:** For instance, promise to stop checking emails after 8 p.m. unless there is a real emergency. Or limit weekend work to rare occasions.
- **Schedule downtime:** Include rest or leisure as a non-negotiable appointment in your weekly planner. Treat it as seriously as a client meeting.
- **Celebrate small positives:** Often, men keep pushing forward without noting what they have accomplished. Pausing to say, "I did well on that project," can fuel healthier motivation.

Finding a healthy approach to ambition means knowing when to push and when to rest. This helps avoid the crash of burnout, which can take weeks or months to recover from.

9. Remote Work Challenges

Working from home (or remotely) might reduce commute times and allow some flexibility, but it can also introduce new forms of stress:

- **Lack of boundary between work and home:** Men might find themselves checking messages at night or on weekends because the office is just a few steps away.
- **Feeling isolated:** Without face-to-face interaction, a person can start feeling detached or lonely. Video calls might not replace real human contact.
- **Overworking:** Some remote workers put in longer hours, hoping to show they are not slacking off. This can lead to fast burnout.

Combat these issues by setting clear work hours and a dedicated workspace if possible. Take real breaks away from the screen, and try to maintain social connections in other ways, like short phone calls or safe meetups if that is an option. Also, watch out for digital overload—spending the entire day on video calls can be more draining than many people expect.

10. Financial Stress at Work

Money issues can add another layer of stress. If a man is worried about paying bills or has debts, he may put up with an unhealthy job or fear asking for better conditions. Some men might work multiple jobs or overtime just to stay afloat. This can lead to chronic exhaustion and a sense of being trapped.

Ideas to handle financial stress linked to work:

- **Check workplace benefits:** Some companies have financial planning tools or savings programs.
- **Budget planning:** Even a basic budget to track income and expenses can bring clarity. Knowing exactly where money goes can reduce the fear of the unknown.

- **Seek professional advice:** Meeting with a financial counselor can help plan debt repayment or smarter spending. This could ease the pressure to work endless hours.
- **Side training:** Gaining a new skill might allow a jump to a better-paying position. Sometimes, short certification courses can raise earning potential in a modest time frame.

Handling financial stress in a practical way can help a man avoid feeling stuck in a toxic job. It can also reduce tension with family members, who might be worried about monthly bills.

---

11. Unexpected Causes of Workplace Tension

Not all job-related stress comes from heavy workloads. Sometimes tension with coworkers or supervisors is the main trigger. Gossip, unclear communication, or favoritism can create a hostile environment. Another overlooked factor is poor leadership at the top. If managers do not know how to delegate properly or keep changing priorities, employees can feel lost.

Less common factors that can build stress:

- **Physical environment:** Flickering lights, poor ventilation, or uncomfortable seating can cause fatigue and mood changes over time.
- **Moral distress:** A man might see unfair policies or harm being done to clients and feel guilty for staying silent.
- **Lack of growth:** Doing the same tasks without any chance to learn something new can lead to boredom and frustration.

Addressing these issues might require open conversations, seeking transfers within the company, or in some cases, leaving for a healthier workplace. Being aware of subtle tensions is helpful so they do not sneak up and compound daily stress.

---

12. Time Management Pitfalls

Poor time management at work can make stress much worse. Some men underestimate how long tasks take, so they scramble at the last minute. Others do not organize their day, letting urgent requests push out important work until late. Over time, this pattern can be exhausting.

Tips to improve time use:

- **Set realistic deadlines:** If a task usually takes three hours, do not schedule it for a one-hour window. Build in a buffer for unforeseen issues.
- **Prioritize daily:** In the morning, list the top two or three tasks that must be done. Focus on them first if possible.
- **Watch for time sinks:** Checking personal social media, random internet browsing, or lengthy casual chats can eat up hours. Track your day to see where time goes.
- **Batch similar tasks:** Handle phone calls or emails in blocks instead of scattering them throughout the day. This reduces the mental cost of switching tasks often.

Better time management can reduce feeling rushed, which in turn lowers stress. It also leaves mental space to handle unplanned problems without total panic.

---

13. The Value of a Support System at Work

Building relationships at work can buffer stress. Having at least one coworker you trust can make a difference. This person can listen, share ideas, or even laugh with you during tough times. Joining or forming a small group of employees who also want a healthier environment can help bring positive change. Sometimes, just knowing you are not alone can ease the mental load.

If the workplace culture is cold or competitive, creating these bonds might be tricky. In that case, looking outside the job for a support system is vital. This could be a spouse, friend, or mental health group. Chatting about problems can bring new views or solutions you have not considered. Also, hearing other people's stories can reduce the feeling that you are the only one struggling.

---

14. Learning to Say "No"

Men who always say "yes" to more duties can burn out fast. While it is good to be helpful, taking on every request might be harmful if it overloads the schedule. Learning to say "no" in a polite, firm way is a key skill.

- **Check your current load:** Before agreeing to a new project, see if you have space in your calendar to do it without harm.

- **Offer alternatives:** If you must say "no," you could suggest another coworker who might handle it, or propose a later date when you have time.
- **Maintain respect:** Use respectful language. You might say, "I'm sorry, but I can't take this on right now because of X project's deadline."
- **Set clear boundaries:** If your boss repeatedly piles on new tasks, schedule a talk to discuss priorities and realistic timelines.

Saying "no" does not make you a bad employee. It often shows you respect the quality of your work and your mental limits. Overcommitting and then performing poorly helps no one.

---

15. Using Breaks and Vacations Wisely

Men sometimes feel guilty taking breaks or using vacation days. But pushing on without rest can lead to burnout, health issues, and bigger mistakes. Breaks are not lazy; they are a practical way to maintain steady performance.

- **Daily breaks:** A short walk or a few minutes of quiet can restore focus. Men who skip lunch to work at their desk might see a drop in afternoon energy.
- **Longer vacations:** A proper vacation allows deeper rest. It also helps clear the mind from daily problems. Some men spend vacations doing chores or remain glued to work emails. That defeats the purpose.
- **Staycations:** Even if you cannot travel, taking time off to rest at home or pursue a personal hobby can refresh the brain and body.

Make a habit of planning time off in advance. Having a vacation on the calendar can give hope during stressful stretches. Also, do not wait for the perfect time—there is rarely a moment at work when everything is calm. Taking breaks proactively shows that you value your long-term health.

---

16. Combating Unfair Self-Talk About Work

Men sometimes set impossible standards, saying, "I should be able to handle all of this without complaint." That kind of self-talk can lock them in a cycle of denial. Over time, they blame themselves for not coping better, which deepens sadness or shame. In reality, some work pressures would overwhelm anyone.

Ways to adjust negative self-talk:

- **Speak to yourself kindly:** If a coworker were going through the same stress, would you tell him he's just weak? Or would you show understanding? Offer yourself the same fairness.
- **List what is in your control:** Focus on what you can change, like time management or talking to a supervisor. Accept that some factors are beyond your power.
- **Acknowledge effort:** Even if results are not perfect, notice times when you are trying your best.
- **Use factual language:** Instead of "I'm failing," say, "I'm behind schedule because the project requirements doubled."

Shifting self-talk can lift some mental weight and open the way to real solutions. It also prevents the trap of feeling like a constant failure.

---

17. Chapter Summary

Work stress is a serious issue that can push men toward sadness or deeper mental health problems. In many cases, men feel they have no choice but to keep going, ignoring warning signs like insomnia, irritability, or a constant sense of dread. But there are practical steps to reduce and handle this pressure. From simple daily habits like micro-breaks and better time management, to more significant decisions like changing jobs, men have options.

This chapter explored many sides of job stress: the hidden traps of modern workplaces, the signs that work is the source of low mood, and the ways it can spill into personal life. We also reviewed less-common strategies, like structured micro-breaks and controlled email use. By combining these tips with clear communication at work, men can protect both their careers and their mental health.

Up next, **CHAPTER 10** will look at **family and relationship pressures**. Challenges at home can be just as intense as those at work. We will discuss how conflicts with partners, children, or relatives can take a toll on a man's well-being, and we will show how to handle these tensions without feeling alone or powerless.

CHAPTER 10: FAMILY AND RELATIONSHIP PRESSURES

Family life can be a source of love and comfort, but it can also bring stress, disagreements, and heavy expectations. Many men feel trapped between work demands and the need to care for their partner, children, or other relatives. In this chapter, we will explore how family and relationship pressures can add to low mood. We will also discuss tactics men can use to handle conflicts in the home, improve communication, and keep close ties healthy. We will look at less obvious points, like how unspoken rules or unbalanced chores can quietly damage mental health. By understanding these pressures more clearly, men can find ways to solve problems in their personal lives without giving up on the people they love.

---

1. Common Relationship Challenges for Men

Men can face various issues in their personal lives that add stress or sadness:

1. **Communication gaps:** Some men find it hard to express emotions. If their partner needs frequent discussions, the man may feel out of his comfort zone.
2. **Financial disagreements:** Money problems can spark fights. A man might feel responsible for providing, or he might argue with a partner about spending choices.
3. **Different parenting styles:** If both parents disagree on rules or discipline, it can create daily tension. This can spill over into blame and guilt.
4. **Role confusion:** Some men grew up seeing one style of father or husband, but modern life might call for a different approach. Adjusting can cause stress if the man is unsure how to act.

These challenges do not mean a relationship is doomed. But if left unaddressed, they can push a man toward isolation, self-doubt, or simmering resentment.

---

2. Why Conflicts at Home Hit Hard

Men often see home as the one place they should be at ease. When trouble arises there, it can feel like there is nowhere to truly relax. Conflicts with a partner might also poke at deeper fears of failure or rejection. If arguments happen often, a man might feel like he cannot ever measure up. He might bottle up his feelings to keep the peace, which can fuel sadness or anger.

Family conflicts can also lead to practical problems:

- **Loss of sleep** from late-night fights.
- **Damage to self-esteem** if harsh words are used.
- **Isolation** if the man avoids family members or friends to keep from discussing problems.

Work life might worsen this tension if a man is already stretched thin. Even positive life events—like the birth of a child—add new responsibilities that can overwhelm an already tired person. Recognizing the emotional impact of home conflicts can help men decide to seek change instead of suffering quietly.

---

3. Hidden Pressures Men Face in Relationships

Some family demands are easy to see, like paying bills or driving kids to school. Others are more subtle:

- **Emotional labor:** This means the mental load of planning events, remembering birthdays, or managing conflicts among relatives. Sometimes men or their partners carry the bulk of this, building resentment.
- **Cultural or generational expectations:** In certain families, men might be expected to always act strong. In others, they might be pushed to show emotions they were never taught to share. Both can be stressful if it conflicts with personal comfort.
- **Blended families:** Men who remarry or have stepchildren might deal with loyalty questions, rules that differ between households, or complicated ex-partner relationships.
- **Elder care:** Taking care of aging parents can add time and emotional strain. Men might feel torn between caring for parents, children, and holding down a job.

These hidden pressures can pile up until they feel overwhelming. A man might not even notice how much he is carrying until he reaches a breaking point.

---

4. Communication Tools for a More Peaceful Home

Talking through issues can reduce misunderstandings and prevent tension from building. Here are simple, practical steps:

1. **Use clear statements:** Instead of saying, "You never help," mention the specific chore or situation. For example, "It would help me if you could handle the dishes after dinner while I put the kids to bed."
2. **Active listening:** Give full attention when your partner speaks. Repeat back what you heard: "So you're saying you feel ignored when I'm on my phone during dinner?" This shows you want to understand.
3. **Schedule check-ins:** Pick a calm time—maybe weekly—to talk about what went well and what was tough. Keep it short but focused. This avoids waiting until a big blow-up forces the issue.
4. **Agree on signals:** If arguments escalate, have a phrase or gesture that means, "We need to pause and cool off." Then resume talking when both are calmer.
5. **Stay solution-focused:** After each discussion, ask, "What can we do about it?" List possible actions. This prevents endless blame.

Communication tools might feel awkward at first if a couple is not used to talking openly. But small improvements can add up, lowering the stress level at home.

---

5. Balancing Family and Work Duties

Men can feel they are in a tug-of-war, trying to meet job demands and also be present at home. This can lead to guilt if work wins over family time, or stress if family needs pull them away from job tasks. To find balance:

- **Set priorities:** Identify which family activities are most important. Maybe attending a child's school event ranks higher than a minor work meeting. Communicate this to a boss if necessary.

- **Work efficiency:** If you can finish tasks faster or negotiate flexible hours, you might have more time for home life.
- **Delegate household tasks:** If finances allow, hire help for cleaning or yard work. If not, see if you can share chores among family members so the load is not all on one person.
- **Quality vs. quantity:** Even if you cannot spend large amounts of time at home, make the time you do have more meaningful. Turn off work notifications, sit down for a family meal, or play a game with your kids without distractions.

It helps to speak openly with your partner about scheduling. If you keep your struggles hidden, resentment might grow. But if you work together, it becomes a team effort to handle demands from both sides.

6. When the Relationship Itself Feels Strained

Sometimes, the core issue is not just work or chores. The relationship itself might be facing deeper problems like lost trust, major differences in goals, or emotional distance. This can cause a man to feel lonely or hopeless, even if he is in a long-term partnership.

Signs that a relationship might be under serious strain:

- Recurring fights that do not resolve, just repeat.
- Feeling indifferent, where one or both partners no longer care to fix problems.
- Contempt, expressed through insults or mocking.
- Total lack of physical or emotional closeness.

In these cases, couple's counseling may be necessary. A trained professional can mediate discussions, help identify root problems, and suggest ways to rebuild respect. It can feel scary to involve a third party, but this step can make a big difference if both partners still want the relationship to succeed.

7. Parenting Worries and Pressures

Raising children brings joy, but it also adds big responsibilities. Men might feel huge pressure to be perfect dads. Mistakes can cause guilt or shame. Other worries include:

- **Discipline disagreements:** If each parent has a different style, kids might get confused or learn to play one parent against the other.
- **Time shortage:** Job demands might reduce the time a father has with his kids. He might feel he is missing out on important milestones.
- **Fear of failing:** Some men worry that if their kids struggle in school or have behavior problems, it reflects badly on them as fathers.
- **Financial load:** Children can be expensive. The father might feel extra weight if he believes he must provide everything.

Parenting stress can lead a man to doubt himself. But no parent is perfect. Admitting that challenges exist is normal. Seeking help from parenting classes or talking to other fathers can ease the sense of going it alone.

---

8. Handling Toxic Family Members

Not all family relationships are loving or supportive. Some men deal with relatives who are overly critical, manipulative, or even abusive. This can trigger or worsen sadness. The idea of cutting ties with family might go against cultural values or personal feelings of duty. However, staying in constant contact with a toxic relative can erode mental well-being.

Steps to handle toxic dynamics:

- **Set boundaries:** Decide what topics are off-limits or how often you will engage. If calls always end in arguments, limit call length or frequency.
- **Seek outside support:** A counselor can guide you in dealing with guilt and teaching firm boundary skills.
- **Use calm responses:** Do not let them pull you into heated fights. If they begin yelling, you can calmly say you will end the call or visit now and talk another time.
- **Know when to step away:** In severe cases, limiting or stopping contact might be the healthiest move. This is a personal choice but should be considered if mental health is at stake.

Guilt may arise, but protecting your own health can be a priority when a family member is truly harmful.

9. Golden Tips for Conflict Resolution at Home

Here are some lesser-discussed methods that can help settle disagreements:

1. **Start with agreement:** Even if you disagree on many points, begin a talk by noting a shared interest. For example, "We both love our child and want them to do well in school." This sets a positive tone.
2. **Write it down:** If verbal arguments keep spiraling, try writing concerns in a short note. Then the other person can read and reply calmly.
3. **Divide the problem:** Large issues, like "We have no time together," can be split into smaller steps. Maybe the first step is 30 minutes of quiet time each evening. Start small and build up.
4. **Take blame out:** Phrases like "You always" or "You never" cause defensiveness. Replace them with "I feel upset when..." or "I need help with..."
5. **Agree on a plan:** End the discussion with a concrete, simple plan. For instance, "We will take turns cooking dinner on weekdays," or "We will have a budget talk every Sunday evening."

Conflict resolution should be aimed at finding a win-win outcome, or at least a fair compromise. This lowers bitterness and can preserve love and respect.

---

10. Dealing with Divorce or Separation

Sometimes, despite best efforts, a relationship may end. This event can deeply affect a man's mental health, especially if children are involved. Men might fear losing daily contact with their kids or worry about finances. Grief, anger, and regret are common emotions during separation.

Ways to reduce emotional fallout:

- **Legal clarity:** Hire a lawyer or mediator who can explain rights and duties. Unclear legal issues can add panic and confusion.
- **Support network:** Confide in close friends or a support group for men going through separation. It helps to share experiences and learn from others.
- **Child-focused approach:** If children are involved, try to keep their routine as stable as possible. Avoid using them as messengers in adult conflicts.
- **Self-care:** Resist the urge to drown feelings in alcohol or risky behavior. Use methods like exercise or counseling to process the pain.

- **Plan forward:** Even if life feels shattered, setting small new goals can restore a sense of direction. This might be a new place to live, a course to learn a skill, or a hobby that brings peace.

Divorce is a major life change, and feeling overwhelmed is normal. However, men who seek help and keep some stability in daily habits usually find they can move toward acceptance and rebuild over time.

---

11. Aging Parents and Family Obligations

Men might find themselves caring for aging parents. This could mean financial help, driving them to medical appointments, or even inviting them to live in the same home. Such responsibility can be emotionally heavy, especially if there are past resentments or a complicated family history.

Helpful strategies:

- **Share tasks with siblings:** If possible, split duties so one person does not carry the entire load. Even small help from others can add relief.
- **Look for community resources:** Many areas have adult day-care centers, home nursing services, or volunteer programs that ease caregiving stress.
- **Emotional acceptance:** Recognize that caring for a parent can be hard and sad at times. It is okay to feel frustrated or mourn the parent's declining health.
- **Set limits:** If a parent is demanding or unkind, decide on how much care you can provide without sacrificing your own well-being. Try to find outside support if it becomes too much.

Caring for aging relatives can bring guilt and stress, but it can also create moments of closeness and understanding. Balancing these sides is a personal process for each man.

---

12. Maintaining Personal Identity

With family pressures, a man can lose sight of his own interests. He might become "Dad," "Husband," or "Son," and nothing else. This can lead to feeling trapped or bored. Maintaining a personal identity is crucial for mental health.

Ways to keep a sense of self:

- **Hobbies:** Reserve at least a small block of time each week for activities you enjoy, whether it is reading, sports, or creating art.
- **Personal goals:** Besides family goals (kids' education, house projects), set at least one individual goal. It might be learning a new skill or saving money for a solo trip.
- **Friends and social groups:** Stay in touch with people who know you outside of family roles. This could be old friends, interest clubs, or online communities.
- **Mindful reflection:** Spend a few minutes thinking about how you feel and what you want in life. Keeping a journal can help track changes and keep personal dreams alive.

Striking a balance between family roles and self-care is not selfish; it often makes a man a better, more present father, partner, or son.

---

13. Supporting Each Other as a Couple

Family stress is not just the man's job to solve. Couples can share the load, which can deepen their bond. Here are ways to build this team approach:

- **Trade tasks:** One partner might handle bills while the other takes care of cooking. This avoids confusion over who does what.
- **Check in emotionally:** Ask your partner how they are coping, and share your own status too. Even five minutes of genuine talk can reconnect you both.
- **Joint planning:** Whether it is budgeting, holiday trips, or kids' schedules, sit down and plan together. When both have input, blame tends to decrease.
- **Appreciation:** Small words of thanks—"I appreciate you picking up groceries"—can go a long way. Feeling valued eases tension.

When both partners treat each other as allies, problems feel more manageable. Teamwork prevents the sense that one person is carrying everything.

14. When Professional Help Is Needed

Family or relationship pressures sometimes reach a point where external support is vital. This can include:

- **Couples therapy:** A counselor helps partners communicate better, sort out old hurts, and create new relationship rules.
- **Family therapy:** Sessions can involve several family members to address group conflicts or patterns.
- **Anger management classes:** If fights become aggressive, a structured program can teach calmer ways to respond.
- **Parenting workshops:** Learning child development basics and discipline methods can reduce confusion and fights over how to raise kids.

Some men hesitate to bring in an outsider, fearing it will expose family problems. But professional help often speeds up solutions that might not appear otherwise. It can also teach new skills to keep the family strong in the long term.

---

15. Handling Relatives Who Judge or Interfere

A man might have well-meaning relatives who try to shape his parenting or marriage. Unwanted advice or criticism can cause stress, especially if those relatives do not respect boundaries. Sometimes, they might even interfere openly, telling the man's partner what to do or scolding children without permission.

Ways to manage interfering relatives:

- **Polite but firm approach:** "Thank you for your concern, but we have decided to do it this way."
- **Unified front with your partner:** Agree beforehand how you will respond if a relative criticizes. If both of you say the same thing, the relative might back down.
- **Know your rights:** You do not have to share every family detail. Keep some topics private if it avoids drama.
- **Limit contact if needed:** If a relative's interference is extreme, reduce visits or set strict visiting rules.

Not everyone in the family will approve of your choices, and that is okay. What matters is protecting your well-being and the harmony of your immediate household.

16. Chapter Summary

Family and relationship pressures can weigh heavily on men, possibly leading to low mood or persistent sadness if they are not addressed. This chapter covered a range of home-based stresses: communication gaps, role confusion, parenting worries, conflicts with partners, toxic relatives, and aging parents. All of these factors can chip away at a man's sense of peace and self-worth.

But there are solid tools for dealing with these challenges. Improved communication, shared responsibilities, healthy boundaries, and joint planning can ease tension in a relationship. Sometimes, professional help—through therapy or classes—offers a more direct path to repair. It is also essential for men to keep their own identity alive by nurturing personal interests and friendships.

Addressing family stress does not mean blaming yourself or others. It means taking honest steps to handle conflicts, speak openly, and build a supportive home environment. Overcoming these hurdles can be a powerful way to protect mental health. It can also bring more closeness and cooperation among partners, children, and other relatives.

In the following chapters, we will look at how to change negative thought patterns, use practical exercises to support well-being, and expand social connections. Step by step, men can learn to manage both home and outer life with greater calm and confidence.

CHAPTER 11: CHANGING NEGATIVE THOUGHT PATTERNS

Some men feel stuck in a cycle of negative thoughts that fuel sadness and low self-esteem. These thoughts might say, "I am no good," "I always fail," or "Nothing will get better." Such thinking can spread to work life, family life, and even personal goals. In this chapter, we will look at how these negative thought patterns form and share practical methods to help men think in more balanced ways. We will cover facts that might not always appear in day-to-day talk, and we will include specific steps to replace hopeless thoughts with clearer, more realistic ideas. By learning to handle negative thinking, men can gain more control over their moods and decisions.

---

1. Why Negative Thoughts Feel So Real

Negative thoughts often feel like concrete facts. When a man repeatedly tells himself, "I always mess up," his mind starts believing this statement as truth. These beliefs can start in childhood, when a boy might get scolded or teased and come to think he deserves the put-downs. They can also form during stressful periods, like a tough job environment or a major life setback.

Many men do not realize that such thoughts can become habits. The brain likes to save energy by reusing the same thinking paths. If those paths are "I'm worthless," the man may accept it without challenge. Over time, this pattern seeps into daily life. He might avoid opportunities, thinking he will fail anyway. Or he might respond angrily to a small mistake, believing it proves he is no good. Recognizing how the brain adopts these beliefs is the first step toward replacing them with more realistic perspectives.

---

2. Common Negative Thinking Styles

Negative thought patterns come in several forms. Below are a few of the most common, along with examples of what they might look like in practice:

1. **All-or-nothing thinking:** A man sees things in black or white terms, such as "If I don't do this perfectly, I'm a complete failure." This ignores middle ground and puts huge pressure on him.
2. **Overgeneralization:** One bad event, like a missed promotion, is used to judge all future events: "I failed once, so I will always fail." This lumps everything into a single defeat.
3. **Mind reading:** The man assumes he knows what others think: "They're talking about me behind my back." He has no proof, but he treats this guess as fact.
4. **Fortune-telling:** He predicts a negative future without evidence: "I'll never be able to learn this skill, so there's no point in trying."
5. **Discounting positives:** Good outcomes are brushed aside as luck or unimportant: "Sure, I got this award, but anyone could have done that."

Spotting these patterns is key. Once a man realizes he is thinking in these ways, he can pause and analyze whether there is any real proof behind the assumption.

---

3. How Negative Thoughts Affect Daily Life

Men who persistently view themselves or their situations as bad may find their behaviors shaped by that mindset. For example:

- **Avoidance:** If a man thinks he is going to fail, he might skip training or not apply for a better job. He is so sure of defeat that he never gives himself a real chance.
- **Mood swings:** Negative beliefs often bring feelings of despair, guilt, or anger. This can strain relationships, since the man may lash out or withdraw.
- **Reduced problem-solving:** If someone believes no solution exists, he might not bother looking for one. This can trap him in ongoing issues.
- **Health issues:** Chronic negative thinking can raise stress levels, which might affect sleep, digestion, and even heart health. Over time, this can lead to more severe problems.

Seeing how negative thinking influences choices can motivate a man to make changes. Recognizing that self-defeating ideas can hold back one's potential is a powerful reason to work on healthier thought patterns.

---

4. The Inner Critic

The "inner critic" is that voice inside the mind that judges actions harshly. It might say, "You're so lazy," or "Everyone else is better than you." This critic can come from past experiences with teachers, parents, or bosses. Over time, the man's own voice starts echoing those old criticisms. The critic might claim to be helpful, pushing the man to do better, but in truth it often tears down confidence.

Ways to manage the inner critic:

- **Notice the critic's tone:** Is it calling you names, exaggerating, or using extreme words like "always" or "never"?
- **Label it as a thought, not truth:** You can say, "I'm hearing the critic again," instead of thinking, "I'm truly worthless." Recognizing that it is just a voice, not reality, gives some distance.
- **Talk back calmly:** Respond with facts or balanced statements: "I made a mistake here, but that does not mean I mess up everything."
- **Seek positive input:** Spend time with supportive people or read encouraging material. This helps offset the negative tape running in your head.

Understanding the critic's origins can also help. Maybe a strict teacher said something years ago that you still repeat. Realizing this can lessen its hold.

---

5. Key Fact: The Brain's Bias for Negativity

Science shows the brain has a built-in tilt toward noticing problems over positives. This was once helpful for survival—our ancestors needed to spot threats quickly. But in modern times, it can lead to constant anxiety or self-doubt. Men might replay a single criticism while ignoring ten compliments they received the same day.

Practical steps to handle negativity bias:

- **Intentional gratitude:** Make it a habit to name a few positive things each day. This balances out the brain's tendency to focus on the bad.
- **List achievements:** Write down things you do well, even if they seem small. Look at this list when negative thoughts arise.

- **Limit negative media:** If watching certain news channels or social media feeds makes you anxious, consider cutting back.
- **Mindful reflection:** Spend a quiet minute noticing what went right in the day. This helps train the brain to see good events too.

By being aware of the brain's tilt, a man can actively work to counter it. He will not become blindly optimistic, but he can develop a fairer view of his life and self.

---

6. Replacing Harmful Thoughts with Balanced Ones

One effective method for changing negative patterns is replacing them with more accurate thoughts. This does not mean lying to yourself with overly bright statements. It means finding a middle path that is realistic. For example:

- **Harmful thought:** "I messed up that meeting. I'm hopeless at my job."
- **Balanced response:** "I struggled in that meeting because I didn't prepare enough. Next time, I can plan better. One bad meeting does not define my entire skill set."

The second thought acknowledges a mistake but stays away from labeling oneself as hopeless. It also suggests a plan for improvement rather than concluding there is no fix. Practicing these replacements takes time, but each attempt forms healthier brain connections.

---

7. The ABC Technique (Adapted from Cognitive Methods)

A simpler approach, often linked to cognitive behavioral principles, is using ABC:

- **A (Activating event):** Something happens, like missing a deadline.
- **B (Belief about the event):** The man might think, "I'm a failure. Everyone will laugh at me."
- **C (Consequence, emotional or behavioral):** He feels ashamed, depressed, or angry.

The step often added is **D (Dispute)**. The man disputes the negative belief: "Is it fair to call myself a failure over one missed deadline? People miss deadlines sometimes. I can learn and do better." By challenging the belief, he can form new outcomes. Then the final step is **E (Effective new thinking)**: "I need to plan my time differently. That does not mean I am a failure as a person."

This technique breaks the chain of automatic negativity. Instead of letting the mind race from event to meltdown, the man steps in to question and reframe.

---

8. Thought Records

A thought record is a tool men can use to keep track of negative thinking and practice turning it around. It involves writing down situations that cause stress or sadness, the thoughts that arise, and how strong the feelings are. Next, the man looks for facts that support or contradict the thoughts. Then he writes a new, more balanced statement. Over time, these records help spot patterns and reduce the hold of harsh beliefs.

Sample template (simplified):

1. **Situation:** "Boss criticized my report."
2. **Thoughts:** "I'm incompetent. He probably hates me."
3. **Emotions:** Anxiety level 8/10, sadness 7/10.
4. **Evidence for:** "He did point out real errors. I made some mistakes."
5. **Evidence against:** "He also said parts of the report were strong. He never said he hates me. This is an assumption."
6. **New thought:** "I need to improve my editing. That does not mean I'm incompetent overall."

Repeating this process builds a habit of questioning snap judgments. Men often find that after a few weeks of doing this, they see improvements in confidence and mood.

---

9. The Role of Self-Talk

Self-talk is the constant narration in your mind. Many men do not even notice it, but it can shape daily experiences. When self-talk is negative—saying things like, "This day is ruined" or "I can't do anything right"—it sets a bleak tone. Positive or balanced self-talk, on the other hand, can keep stress in check.

- **Examples of healthy self-talk:**
  - "This situation is tough, but I can handle it step by step."
  - "I made a mistake, but I can fix it or learn from it."
  - "Let me focus on what I can control right now."

If negative self-talk is deeply ingrained, writing down a few helpful phrases and reading them daily might help. Over time, the mind absorbs these statements more easily and starts using them in stressful moments.

---

10. Breaking the "Yes, But" Habit

Sometimes men try to challenge negative thoughts but quickly block themselves with a "Yes, but..." statement. For instance, "Yes, I did well on that project, but it was an easy task." This denies any benefit of acknowledging success and keeps negativity in place. Such disclaimers can be subtle, but they undercut all positive progress.

Steps to stop it:

- **Pause after "Yes."** Let yourself accept the good fact first. "Yes, I did well on that project." Full stop.
- **Delete "but."** Replace it with "and." If you must add a second idea, say, "Yes, it was an easy task, and I still put in effort."
- **Celebrate small successes:** Let them exist in your mind without being overshadowed by disclaimers. Small wins build a sense of competence.

Ending the "Yes, but" habit might feel odd at first, but it trains your mind to be fair and let in well-earned credit for efforts.

---

11. Using Visual Reminders

Visual cues can help men remember to stop negative thoughts in their tracks. This might mean placing a note on a computer screen saying, "Question the critic," or wearing a small wristband that signals, "Check your thinking." Each time you see it, you remind yourself to check if your mind is drifting into harsh or inaccurate territory.

Some men choose a specific object, like a small stone or coin, to keep in a pocket. Each time they touch it, they do a quick mental check: "What's my mood? Am I being overly negative?" This trick can be powerful because it pairs a physical action with the mental step of reflection.

12. Self-Compassion: A Different Approach

Though some men think being kind to oneself is "soft," research shows self-compassion can reduce harsh criticism and improve overall resilience. Self-compassion means treating yourself as you would treat a good friend. If a friend said, "I messed up. I'm useless," you would likely offer understanding and remind them of their strengths. Doing this for yourself can ease the sting of negative thoughts.

- **Short technique:** When feeling down, say, "I'm having a hard time. This is part of being human. May I be kinder to myself in this moment." Even if it feels odd, it can soften harsh self-blame.
- **Acknowledging feelings:** Let yourself say, "It's normal to feel bad about this mistake, but it does not define me." Accepting the emotion without letting it define your identity allows you to move forward.

Self-compassion does not mean avoiding responsibility. It simply means not beating yourself up while you try to improve.

13. Group Support for Negative Thinking

Talking to others who struggle with similar thought patterns can be eye-opening. Men's support groups or online forums can provide a sense of connection and shared tips. Hearing how another man challenged his all-or-nothing thinking might spark new ideas for you. Additionally, giving support to others can reinforce positive thinking in yourself.

If group settings feel awkward, even having one trusted friend to talk to can help. Explain that you are working on cutting back negative thoughts and see if they can provide honest feedback when they notice you talking yourself down. Sometimes an outside perspective is what we need to spot hidden patterns.

14. Physical Links to Negative Thinking

It might seem surprising, but the body can either fuel or reduce negative thoughts. For instance:

- **Lack of sleep** can make thoughts more negative. The tired brain struggles with emotional balance, turning minor bumps into big worries.
- **High stress hormones** from overwork or poor diet can lower mood and encourage bleak thinking.
- **Lack of exercise** can reduce the flow of feel-good chemicals in the brain, making negativity easier to take hold.

These factors show why a balanced lifestyle—covered in previous chapters about physical health—can play a key role. When men take care of their body, they give their mind a better base to fight negativity.

---

15. Changing the Story You Tell Yourself

We all have a mental "story" we tell about who we are and what our life is like. Men with negative views might define themselves as "the loser," "the unlucky one," or "the guy who always messes up." This story then filters how they see new events, ignoring anything that does not fit the negative label.

Ways to rewrite your story:

1. **List past successes:** Notice times you overcame problems or learned new skills. Incorporate these into your identity. You are also "the guy who can adapt" or "the man who bounced back before."
2. **Look at the big picture:** If you have had 10 jobs, maybe 2 ended badly, but 8 were fine. Recognize the overall record rather than focusing on just the failures.
3. **Adopt a growth mindset:** Instead of "I'm bad at talking to people," shift to "I'm still learning to communicate better. I can get better with practice."
4. **Practice rewriting:** If you catch yourself saying, "I'm an unlucky person," pause and try to phrase it differently: "I had a setback, but I can find new opportunities."

This mental reframing does not mean ignoring real problems. It just means not letting them overshadow who you are at your core.

16. Professional Help and Cognitive Methods

Sometimes self-guided efforts might not be enough. If negative thinking is deep-rooted, a counselor or therapist who specializes in cognitive approaches can guide you more effectively. They can help identify thought distortions, develop customized replacement thoughts, and keep track of progress over time.

Benefits of professional support:

- **Expert perspective:** A trained person can see patterns you might miss and offer new strategies.
- **Accountability:** Regular sessions ensure you keep practicing, rather than forgetting after a few days.
- **Deeper exploration:** You can explore past events or unresolved issues that feed current negativity. A professional can guide you through this in a safe way.

Therapy is not about "fixing" a broken person. It is about learning skills to handle thoughts and emotions. For many men, even a few sessions can spark lasting change in how they approach negative thinking.

---

17. Practical Daily Habits

Changing thought patterns does not happen overnight. Building consistent habits helps:

1. **Morning check:** As soon as you wake up, notice your first thoughts. If they are negative, counter them with a simple balanced statement.
2. **Midday reflection:** Set an alarm or reminder to pause for 1 minute, ask how your thinking has been, and adjust if needed.
3. **End-of-day review:** Jot down one negative thought you had, the evidence for or against it, and a better replacement thought.
4. **Brief relaxation breaks:** A calm mind is less likely to spiral into gloom. Try 30 seconds of slow breathing every couple of hours.

Over weeks and months, these small actions reinforce new patterns. They help men become more aware of their mental habits and gradually adopt clearer thinking.

18. Chapter Summary

Negative thought patterns can drag men into deeper sadness, reduce confidence, and limit opportunities. Yet, these patterns are not fixed in stone. By pinpointing common thinking errors, challenging the inner critic, and using structured techniques like ABC or thought records, men can shift toward healthier views of themselves and their futures.

Replacing harmful labels with balanced ones allows men to see mistakes as learning experiences instead of final judgments. Tools like mindful self-talk, self-compassion, and group support can further ease the grip of negativity. It is also important to remember the brain's natural tilt toward scanning for trouble. By actively feeding the mind with realistic positives, men can gradually break the cycle of gloom.

In the next chapter, we will explore **practical daily exercises** that men can use to support mental well-being. These activities, when combined with healthier thinking habits, form a strong foundation for managing sadness and building a more stable mood.

CHAPTER 12: PRACTICAL DAILY EXERCISES

Along with changing negative thought patterns, men can benefit from simple daily exercises that boost emotional stability and lower stress. These are not meant to be magical fixes. Instead, they serve as steady support for overall well-being, like having a mental gym routine. In this chapter, we will lay out several specific activities and show how to fit them into a busy schedule. We will also point out facts that go beyond the usual "just do breathing exercises" advice, giving men more tools to build real progress. By trying some or all of these exercises, men can discover what suits their lifestyle best.

---

1. Breathing Drills for Quick Stress Relief

One of the most straightforward methods for calming nerves is controlled breathing. It can be done in seconds and does not require special equipment.

- **Box breathing:** Inhale through the nose for a slow count of 4, hold for 4, exhale for 4, hold for 4. Repeat this pattern a few times. It can reset an anxious mind.
- **4-7-8 method:** Inhale for a count of 4, hold for 7, exhale for 8. This pattern is said to slow heart rate and soothe tension.

Men can use these drills in various settings—before a tense meeting, after an argument, or any time stress spikes. By focusing on the count, the mind has less room for racing thoughts. Over time, this habit can reduce overall stress levels.

---

2. The Power of Journaling

Writing is a direct way to process thoughts and feelings that might otherwise swirl in the mind.

- **Stream-of-consciousness writing:** Set a timer for 5 or 10 minutes and write down whatever comes to mind without stopping. It often reveals hidden worries or ideas.
- **Topic-focused journaling:** Pick a theme, such as work stress or family relationships. Spend a few minutes describing current worries, possible solutions, or next steps.

- **Positive reflection:** End each entry by listing at least one positive point from the day. This balances the focus if the journal entry was full of problems.

Men who keep a regular journal often say it helps them see patterns in their behavior or moods. It also clears mental clutter, creating space for calmer thinking.

---

3. Physical Releases of Tension

Stress often builds up physically in the body—tight shoulders, clenched jaw, or headaches. Releasing this tension can lead to mental relief.

- **Progressive muscle tightening and releasing:** Start with the feet, tense the muscles for a few seconds, then release. Move upward through calves, thighs, stomach, arms, and face. It teaches the difference between tension and relaxation.
- **Shaking it out:** Stand up and gently shake your arms, hands, legs, or shoulders for 30 seconds. Some men find this surprisingly refreshing, as if shaking off stress.
- **Self-massage:** Roll a tennis ball under your foot or along your back against a wall. This can help loosen knots. It also gives you a chance to breathe and focus on your body's sensations.

These actions can be done in short breaks throughout the day. They are quick to do but can lower overall stress load, especially when used often.

---

4. Structured Mindful Moments

Mindfulness is not just about meditation. It is about paying attention to the present in a non-judgmental way. Small mindful moments scattered throughout the day can help men stay grounded.

- **Senses check:** Pause and note what you see, hear, feel, smell, and taste. This draws the mind into "now" instead of worrying about the future or past.
- **Slow walk:** If you walk from one place to another, focus on each step—the pressure on your feet, the rhythm of breathing, the breeze on your skin. This short practice can transform a routine walk into a calming break.

- **One-task focus:** When doing a simple job (like washing dishes), concentrate fully on it. Notice the water temperature, the smell of soap, the feel of dishes. If the mind drifts, bring it back to the task.

Over time, mindfulness can improve attention and reduce stress. It teaches the mind to catch runaway thoughts and return to calmer states.

---

5. Building a Personal Morning Routine

How a man starts his day can set the tone for hours ahead. A personal morning routine can include small exercises or rituals that prepare both mind and body.

1. **Hydration:** Drink a glass of water soon after waking up. This helps the body recover from nighttime water loss and can spark alertness.
2. **Stretch or light movement:** Spending 5–10 minutes on gentle stretches or a few squats can wake up stiff muscles and promote blood flow.
3. **Brief mindfulness or prayer:** Take a quiet moment to think of what you are grateful for or set a clear intention for the day.
4. **Plan the day's focus:** Pick one or two tasks that must get done. This keeps the mind from feeling scattered.

Men do not need an hour-long process. Even a short, consistent routine can reduce morning rush stress and boost energy for the day.

---

6. Goal-Setting Exercises

Setting goals is more than just making a wish list. Specific exercises can help men organize their aims and keep motivation steady.

- **SMART goals:** Write goals that are Specific, Measurable, Achievable, Relevant, and Time-bound. For example, "I want to jog for 15 minutes, 3 times a week, for the next month."
- **Daily check-ins:** Each morning or evening, quickly review progress. This keeps goals from slipping away in busy schedules.
- **Adjustment time:** If a goal becomes too easy or too hard, tweak it. Maybe jogging time should increase if it feels effortless. Or if it is too hard to manage 3 times a week, reduce it to 2 but stay consistent.

- **Reward strategy:** Set a small reward for reaching milestones, such as treating yourself to a favorite snack or a fun book. This positive reinforcement can build momentum.

By turning goal-setting into a clear exercise, men can track achievements and build self-confidence step by step.

---

7. Strengthening Social Ties

Some men might overlook the importance of consistent social contact. Regular interaction can lift mood and ease sadness.

- **Short daily chats:** Even a quick phone call or message to a friend helps maintain connections.
- **Shared activities:** Plan simple meetups, like walking together or watching a sports game. Doing something side-by-side can reduce pressure to talk about deep issues but still foster closeness.
- **Community involvement:** Volunteering or joining local clubs can create a sense of purpose. It also exposes a man to new people, reducing isolation.
- **Social check-in list:** If you keep track of close friends or relatives, you might remember to touch base regularly. This is useful if you tend to forget when busy.

Each week, set aside a little time to maintain relationships. This is an exercise in staying connected to others, which supports emotional health.

---

8. Daily Gratitude Practice

Gratitude is not about ignoring problems. It is about noticing what is still good around us, which can balance negative news or setbacks.

- **Gratitude list:** Before bed, list three things you are thankful for. They can be simple: a comfy bed, a good meal, or a kind gesture from someone.
- **Focus on details:** Instead of saying, "I'm thankful for my family," try to be specific: "I'm thankful my brother called today to check on me."
- **Reflect on personal traits:** You can also thank yourself for qualities like patience, persistence, or creativity. Acknowledging one's own positive traits can lessen self-criticism.

- **Share gratitude:** If you feel comfortable, tell someone you appreciate them. This can deepen bonds and spread positivity.

Over time, a habit of gratitude can shift the mind's default setting from "What's wrong?" to "What's also good?"

---

9. Short Physical Workouts

Exercise does not have to be long or extreme to improve mood. Even small workouts can release endorphins that reduce stress.

- **Micro-exercises:** Between tasks, do a quick set of push-ups, sit-ups, or squats. A single set can raise the heart rate and reset the mind.
- **Desk stretches:** Many men spend hours sitting. Every hour, take 1 minute to stand, roll the shoulders, stretch the neck, or do a few calf raises.
- **Ten-minute daily routine:** Pick simple moves—like jumping jacks, lunges, or planks—and do them for 10 minutes. It is enough to wake up the body and mind.
- **Group workouts:** If possible, join a friend for a walk or a short run. This adds a social element and boosts motivation.

Combining short bursts of exercise throughout the day can keep energy levels steadier and maintain a better mood, even with a busy lifestyle.

---

10. Creative Outlets

Expressing feelings through creative means can calm the mind and release built-up emotions. Some men may think creativity is only for artists, but it can be very simple.

- **Sketching or doodling:** Draw random shapes or scenes. This can relax the brain, much like daydreaming.
- **Playing with words:** Write short poems, songs, or funny rhymes. It does not need to be high art; it is about expression.
- **Handicrafts or small building projects:** Working with your hands, whether it is creating a small wood item or painting a model, can focus your thoughts on the present.

- **Music interaction:** Even humming or playing a simple instrument can shift your mood. Some men find rhythm-based activities, like drumming, especially satisfying.

The point is to engage in an activity that allows some form of self-expression or flow. It does not have to be perfect or shared with others. The act itself can be soothing.

---

11. Digital Breaks and Screen Time Control

Too many hours on phones, tablets, or computers can sap mental energy. Short breaks can help.

- **Scheduled offline times:** Decide on specific hours (like 8–9 p.m.) when you avoid all screens. Use that time to read a book, talk to family, or simply rest.
- **App blockers:** Some apps can limit social media usage. If you tend to scroll mindlessly, these tools can remind you to do something else.
- **Blue light filters:** If you must use screens at night, use a blue light filter or night mode to reduce sleep disruption.
- **Mindful scrolling:** If you catch yourself scrolling without purpose, pause. Ask, "Is this helping me, or making me feel worse?"

By reducing mindless screen use, men can reclaim time for better self-care and reduce negative mental clutter that comes from random online content.

---

12. Nightly Wind-Down Routine

Ending the day in a calm state can make sleep more restful and prepare the mind to handle tomorrow's challenges.

- **Dim the lights:** Lower light levels 30 minutes before bed. Harsh lighting can trick the brain into staying alert.
- **Soothing sounds or music:** Some men play soft music or nature sounds to ease into relaxation.
- **Gentle stretching:** Simple poses or light yoga can relieve tension in the back, shoulders, and neck before lying down.

- **Grateful reflection:** Revisit a simple gratitude list or a few positive moments of the day to shift the mind away from worries.

These small steps signal to the body and mind that it is time to relax. Men who keep a steady bedtime routine often report better sleep quality, which leads to improved mood during waking hours.

13. Habit Stacking

An easy way to build these exercises into daily life is "habit stacking." This means attaching a new activity to an existing habit. For instance:

- **After brushing teeth:** Do a short mindful check, asking how you feel today.
- **Before lunchtime:** Perform a 2-minute stretch or breathing drill.
- **After parking the car at home:** Take 30 seconds to shake out tension and mentally shift from work to personal time.
- **Before showering:** Write a quick note in a journal or update a goal checklist.

By pairing new exercises with ingrained routines, men do not have to rearrange their entire schedule. The existing habit triggers the new one, making it easier to stick to over time.

14. Dealing with Resistance and Slip-Ups

Even with the best plans, men may skip exercises when tired, busy, or discouraged. That is normal.

- **Expectation check:** Building a new habit takes time. Do not expect perfection immediately.
- **Plan for obstacles:** If you know a busy morning is coming, pick a shorter exercise or do it the night before.
- **Forgive yourself for mistakes:** If you forget to journal one day, do not abandon the habit. Just resume it the following day.
- **Track small wins:** Each time you complete an exercise, mentally note it. Over a week, you might see you managed it 5 out of 7 days, which is progress.

Consistency grows through patience and adjusting to real-life demands. A slip does not cancel the benefits of what you have already done.

15. Mixing and Matching Methods

Not every exercise will fit every man's life. Some might love journaling, while others find they prefer short physical workouts. Testing different activities and mixing what works best can create a personal "mental fitness" routine.

Possible combos:

- **Morning:** Short stretching + a gratitude statement.
- **Lunch break:** Quick breathing drill + 5-minute walk.
- **Evening:** Light journaling + 2 minutes of muscle relaxation.

As life situations change, men can also swap out exercises. The key is to keep something in place for daily mental care. Even small actions done regularly have a compound effect over time.

16. Community or Family Involvement

Sometimes involving a friend or family member in these exercises can boost motivation.

- **Partner routine:** Do a brief evening stretch together or share gratitude points before sleep.
- **Buddy check-ins:** Text a friend daily about which exercises you did. It can be as simple as a thumbs-up emoji.
- **Family walks:** If you have children, a short daily walk can be a shared activity, mixing exercise with bonding.
- **Group events:** Check if there are local meetups for short workouts or mindfulness sessions. Doing it with others can reduce loneliness.

Shared routines might also improve relationships, turning self-care into a bonding opportunity.

17. Measuring Progress Gently

Unlike weight loss or other clear measures, mental well-being can be subtle. Men can create simple ways to track how they feel:

- **Mood scale:** Each day, rate your mood from 1 to 10. Over weeks, see if there is a pattern of improvement.
- **Stress diary:** Mark daily stress on a scale or with a color code. Check whether daily exercises lead to fewer red (high-stress) days.
- **Sleep quality:** Note how many hours you slept and whether you woke up feeling rested. Some men find better sleep after doing certain activities regularly.
- **Feedback from others:** Pay attention if friends or family mention you seem calmer or more positive.

Progress may be slow or come in small increments. Checking these trends can confirm that the effort is paying off, even if it is not dramatic every day.

---

18. Chapter Summary

Practical daily exercises can reduce sadness and steady a man's emotional health. Whether it is controlled breathing, journaling, light workouts, or short mindful breaks, these methods offer simple but impactful tools. The idea is not to cram every activity into your schedule at once. Instead, pick one or two that seem most useful, practice them regularly, and observe the effect on your mood and stress.

Over time, men can build a personal toolkit of exercises to handle various challenges—be it job stress, family tension, or recurring negative thoughts. This chapter outlined ways to insert these practices smoothly into a busy day, from morning routines to bedtime wind-downs. By trying different options, men can discover which ones fit best, then adjust as life changes. The cumulative benefit of these small steps can be large, improving mood, energy, and overall outlook.

In the next two chapters, we will talk about **building strong friendships** and **setting goals for improvement.** These are further ways men can support long-term well-being, making sure they do not feel alone or uncertain about future directions.

CHAPTER 13: BUILDING STRONG FRIENDSHIPS

Friendships can bring a lot of meaning to a man's life. Close friends can share good times, offer support in tough moments, and give honest feedback when we make poor choices. Sadly, many men struggle to find or keep strong friendships. Some feel unsure about reaching out, while others might think they have no time to meet people outside work. This chapter will talk in clear detail about how men can form and maintain positive bonds. We will look at everyday steps for breaking the ice, building trust, and handling common problems that arise among friends.

Many men feel that having friends is nice but not essential. Research, however, shows that people with stable, long-term friendships often report better mental health. They feel more confident about sharing concerns, and they usually have someone who can step in and help them problem-solve. In earlier chapters, we looked at how social support can lower sadness and stress. Now, we will focus on practical methods to make such support a part of everyday life.

---

1. Why Friend Connections Matter

Friendships are about having someone outside your family or romantic relationship who can see you in a real way. These friendships can reduce the load of daily stress, because you do not have to face everything on your own. When something good happens, friends cheer us on. When something bad happens, they offer comfort or solutions. This sense of understanding can lessen the feeling that nobody knows what we are going through.

Also, having friends gives us a place to test new ideas or share personal stories. If a man is thinking about a career change, a friend can give honest advice. If a man is dealing with sadness, a friend might point him to resources or share personal experiences. Friends also help us get out of our own heads. By talking to someone else, we can see different viewpoints that we might miss on our own.

Men who have at least one close friend often feel less isolated. They know there is a person who will answer their call or text in times of need. Even a short chat can ease tension. On top of that, friends can motivate healthier habits. If a friend wants to exercise regularly, we might join him and stay more consistent than if we tried alone. In all these ways, strong friendships can raise a man's sense of well-being.

2. Understanding the Difference Between Acquaintances and Close Friends

Not all friendships are the same. Some people in our lives are more like acquaintances or casual friends. They might be neighbors, old classmates, or coworkers we see often. We exchange small talk or polite greetings. We might chat about surface-level topics like sports or weekend plans, but we do not feel safe sharing deeper thoughts or fears.

Close friends, on the other hand, are those we trust on a personal level. We feel comfortable telling them about mistakes or worries, and they can do the same with us. Close friendships usually develop over time. Trust and closeness do not appear overnight. They grow as two people share more of themselves and feel accepted in return. Most men do not need a large number of close friends; even one or two can make a big difference.

It is also normal for a friendship to start as casual and deepen with repeated interactions. For instance, two coworkers who only talked about job tasks might bond by discovering shared interests, like a favorite hobby. Over time, they might meet outside of work, talk about family stories, and become more open with each other. Recognizing these levels helps men see that they do not have to jump straight to a deep friendship. Sometimes, consistent small steps can gradually build a closer bond.

---

3. Overcoming Shyness or Social Fear

A major barrier for some men is shyness or social fear. They might worry about being judged or rejected. They could also feel uncomfortable in group settings. If these feelings are strong, reaching out can seem too risky. But hiding from all social events usually feeds loneliness. When men accept that a bit of anxiety is normal, they can take small steps to move past it.

- **Start small:** Rather than attending a large party, look for smaller gatherings or invite one person for coffee. Fewer people can mean less pressure.
- **Prepare topics:** Think of two or three simple things to talk about, like a local event or a funny story. This can stop awkward silence.

- **Use body language:** Make gentle eye contact, nod when listening, and keep your arms uncrossed. This invites the other person to continue speaking.
- **Target shared interests:** It feels easier to talk about a shared hobby. If you both like sports, technology, or a certain style of music, that is a natural way to bond.

Men who feel serious social anxiety might consider professional help or a support group. But many can start with small, repeated practice. Each positive encounter can build confidence. Over time, these small victories reduce the fear of meeting new people.

---

4. Tools for Making New Connections

In the past, men formed friendships mostly through school, neighborhoods, or the military. Today's world can feel more scattered, especially if we move to different cities or work from home. Fortunately, there are still ways to find new people with similar interests.

- **Community events:** Local community centers, libraries, or gyms often hold group activities. Signing up for a class or workshop is a simple way to meet others who share that interest.
- **Sports leagues or clubs:** Many areas have casual sports teams that do not require expert skills. It could be a pick-up basketball group, a softball league, or a weekly soccer match. Exercise plus socializing is a strong combo.
- **Online platforms:** Websites or social apps designed for meeting people can help. Some are specific to shared hobbies, like running or gaming. While online connections might feel less personal at first, they can lead to real-life friendships if both sides are open to it.
- **Work buddies:** Jobs can be a starting point for friendship. If you share lunch breaks or projects, you can gradually find common ground. Inviting a coworker to grab a coffee after work might start a deeper connection.

These methods might require stepping out of a comfort zone. But men who try them regularly often meet people they would never have encountered otherwise. A key tip is consistency: going more than once to the same group or activity gives you a better chance to get to know folks over time.

5. Maintaining Friendships Across Distance

Modern life sometimes scatters friends to different cities or countries. A man's best buddy from college might live hundreds of miles away, or a close coworker might move to another state. Long-distance friendships need extra care to keep them active.

- **Regular check-ins:** A quick phone call, video chat, or text can keep both sides updated on life changes. Even short messages can say, "I'm thinking of you."
- **Plan visits:** If possible, schedule a trip or invite them to stay with you. A weekend together every year or two can keep the friendship from fading.
- **Online shared activities:** Watch the same movie or sports event at the same time while chatting on the phone or through messages. Or play an online game together. This recreates the sense of hanging out.
- **Accept changes:** People's lives evolve. They might get new jobs, families, or interests. Stay open to how the relationship might shift. A good friend might not talk every week, but the bond can stay strong if both sides make an effort.

Long-distance friendship might not be the same as seeing someone often, but it can still be real and supportive. It often depends on both sides being willing to communicate and put in the time.

---

6. Handling Conflict or Misunderstandings

No friendship is perfect. People have differences in personality, opinions, or how they view the world. Sometimes, conflict arises due to a small misunderstanding or a misread text. Men who want to keep a strong friendship should learn basic conflict resolution skills.

1. **Address the issue:** Do not let anger or hurt feelings fester. Calmly bring up the problem: "I felt upset when you did this. Can we talk about it?"
2. **Listen:** Let the other person explain their side. Maybe they did not realize how their words affected you. Or maybe you misunderstood something.
3. **Stay respectful:** Attacking or insulting only leads to more anger. Speak about behaviors rather than labeling a person's character.
4. **Find a middle ground:** If there is a way to meet halfway, suggest it. Or if you made a mistake, own up to it and say how you plan to avoid it again.

5. **Move forward:** Once resolved, try not to keep bringing it up. Friendships grow stronger when both parties show respect and forgiveness.

Some disagreements might be big enough to end a friendship, but in many cases, open and honest dialogue can fix the problem. Even best friends do not see eye to eye on everything. The key is how both handle these rough patches.

---

7. Being Supportive Without Fixing Everything

Sometimes, men hesitate to talk about their problems. They might worry their friend will try to fix or solve all issues, or they might fear judgment. A good friend offers support in a way that respects the other person's need for understanding. This means listening carefully, asking questions, and only giving advice if the friend seems open to it.

- **Active listening:** Let the friend speak without interruption. Make eye contact and nod to show you are paying attention.
- **Ask if they want feedback:** "Do you want my opinion, or do you just want to vent?" This shows respect.
- **Avoid judging:** Try not to jump to "You should have done this instead." Focus on understanding first.
- **Offer practical help:** If they have a specific need, like help with moving or moral support at an event, see if you can pitch in. Actions can speak louder than words.

Men sometimes worry about stepping on each other's personal space. Asking before offering advice can ease that concern. Also, offering quiet, steady support can do more good than a long lecture or immediate solutions.

---

8. When Friendships Change or Fade

Not all friendships last forever. Some fade naturally as people move, start different jobs, or develop new lifestyles. This is not always a negative event; sometimes, it is just a natural shift. However, it can feel sad or confusing if a man values a relationship that the other person has allowed to drift.

- **Accept normal life changes:** People get married, switch careers, or discover new hobbies. These shifts can pull them in different directions. It does not always mean they dislike you.
- **Check in:** If you sense distance, reach out gently. Ask how they have been. If the response is cold or they do not reply, you might have to accept that the friendship is no longer the same.
- **Stay open for reconnection:** Some old friends come back into our lives later, when the timing works better. Leaving the door open can bring a pleasant surprise in the future.
- **Grieve the loss:** It is okay to feel sad if a once-close friend seems to vanish. That hurt can be real. Talking to someone else about it can help you accept and move on.

Letting go of a friendship can free up emotional space for forming new bonds. Holding tight to someone who has clearly moved on usually creates frustration or self-doubt. It is often healthier to accept the new reality and remember the good times with no bitterness.

---

9. The Role of Trust and Honesty

Trust is what turns a casual contact into a meaningful friend. If you share personal details, you hope the other person will keep them private and not laugh behind your back. Likewise, a friend might trust you with their secrets or vulnerabilities. Breaking that trust can harm the relationship badly, so it is important to handle it with care.

- **Keep confidential matters private:** If your friend tells you something sensitive, do not share it with others.
- **Follow through on promises:** If you say you will help them with something, do it. This shows that your word matters.
- **Admit mistakes:** If you accidentally reveal something or do not keep your promise, apologize sincerely and see if you can repair the damage.
- **Be genuine:** Try not to put on a show or pretend to be someone you are not. Authenticity over time builds trust.

Honesty can also mean telling a friend when you think they are making a poor choice. That is usually hard, but if you do it kindly and for their own good, it can strengthen the bond in the long run.

10. Joining Groups for Shared Interests

One easy path for making friends is to join a group related to something you like. This might mean a hiking club, a cooking class, a book club, or a weekly gaming night. When men meet through shared interests, they have a built-in topic to discuss, which makes breaking the ice much simpler than trying to chat with random strangers.

Such groups also let you see the same faces again and again. This repeated contact helps people get familiar with each other naturally. Over a few sessions, you might realize you connect well with someone in the group. That can lead to exchanging phone numbers or meeting outside the group. In time, you could become good friends.

Some men fear group settings, worrying they might not fit in or that everyone else will already know each other. In reality, many group members welcome new participants because they are also looking for connections. Feeling some nervousness is normal, but taking that step can pay off with friends who share your enthusiasm for a certain interest.

11. Checking Your Own Behaviors

Sometimes, we must look in the mirror if we want stronger friendships. A man might say he cannot keep friends, but maybe he is canceling plans too often or always complaining. Being aware of our own habits and how they affect others can open the door to better bonds.

- **Reliability:** Show up on time, or let people know if you will be late. Avoid being the person who bails at the last minute.
- **Positive attitude:** Everyone has bad days, but constant negative talk can drive people away. Try to talk about good things too.
- **Conversation balance:** Let the other person speak. Do not dominate the conversation with your issues.
- **Kindness and courtesy:** Simple politeness, like thanking someone for their time or offering to pay your share, shows respect.

By spotting small lapses in our behavior, we can fix them and see improvements in how others respond. Sometimes, men only need to tweak one or two habits to find themselves being invited out more and forming deeper friendships.

---

12. Helping Each Other Grow

True friends can do more than just hang out. They can motivate each other toward better habits, new skills, or personal development. For example, if you want to start exercising, a friend can be your workout partner. If you plan to change jobs, a friend might introduce you to helpful contacts or give feedback on your resume.

In this way, friendship becomes a source of growth. You see your friend making progress, and it pushes you to do the same. Men who want supportive friendships should also offer that same level of support in return. If your friend is learning a new language or tackling a course, check in to see how it is going. Encourage them. Sharing success stories can keep both sides motivated.

This is not about forced competition. It is about friendly backing. The friend is not trying to outdo you, and you are not trying to look better than them. Instead, you both want each other to succeed. Over time, these shared efforts can deepen respect and loyalty.

---

13. Getting Past Awkward Starts

Making friends as an adult can feel awkward at first. We might be used to childhood or teenage friendships that formed automatically in school. As grown-ups, we must be more active in seeking friends. This can feel strange. You might wonder how to approach someone you have seen at the gym for a month but never spoken to.

- **Start with a simple greeting:** A short "Hey, how's it going?" can open the door. If they seem open to talking, ask a small question like, "How was your workout?" or "Have you tried this machine before?"
- **Look for a small link:** Notice if they wear a shirt with a band you like, or if they talk about a show you have watched. That is your next topic to keep the conversation moving.

- **Offer your name:** If the chat goes well, say, "By the way, I'm [Your Name]." That can prompt them to share their name too. Names help move someone from stranger to acquaintance.
- **Exchange details:** If you have a good talk, consider saying, "We should catch up again sometime. Maybe after next week's class?" Suggest exchanging numbers or social media if it feels right.

Yes, it can be uncomfortable. But many people are open to new friends and welcome a polite approach. The worst that happens is they do not respond well, and you simply move on. The best that happens is you build a lasting connection.

---

14. Overcoming Competitive Impulses

Men sometimes feel a need to compete with their friends. They might compare salaries, physical shape, or romantic success. Healthy competition can be fun if both sides enjoy it, like trying to see who can run a 5K faster. But if the competition turns sour or leads to envy, it can hurt the friendship.

- **Focus on shared enjoyment:** If you both like the same sport, cheer each other on rather than always trying to show who is better.
- **Share successes:** If your friend has a big win at work, be happy for them. Try not to view it as a threat to your own success.
- **Manage pride:** If you do well, share it without belittling your friend. Gloating can breed resentment.
- **Look at your own goals:** If envy keeps surfacing, ask yourself if you are unhappy in some part of your life. Then work on that rather than blaming your friend's success.

A sense of support is crucial in strong friendships. If you find yourself always trying to one-up the other person, it might mean you are insecure about something. Working on that insecurity can lead to healthier friend connections.

---

15. Including Partners and Family

Many adult men have partners, children, or other family members who also need their time. This can make friendship feel like an extra chore. But it can help to combine social life with family life at times. For example, invite a friend and his family over for a barbecue or a simple gathering. That way, you do not have to split time between family and friends. Your partner might also build a friendship with your friend's partner.

For single friends, be mindful that they might not want to be the "third wheel" in your family events, so consider meeting them for coffee or a shared activity. Balancing these factors shows that you value your friend while respecting your commitments at home. Openly communicating about scheduling can stop misunderstandings. Let your friend know that weekends are busy with kids, but you can meet on a weeknight for a short hangout.

---

16. Looking Out for Each Other's Well-Being

Friends can sometimes see red flags in us before we notice them ourselves. If you see your friend showing signs of deep sadness, high stress, or destructive habits, you might be the first person to bring it up. This can be an awkward conversation, but it could be the nudge that helps them get help.

- **Pick a calm moment:** Ask if they have been feeling okay. Mention changes you have noticed in their behavior.
- **Offer help:** Suggest talking it out further or seeing a professional. Provide phone numbers or websites if they seem open to it.
- **Stay supportive:** If they push you away at first, do not give up. Check in gently again later.
- **Protect your own health:** If their problems are too big for you to handle alone, encourage them to seek expert guidance. Do not try to bear their entire burden on your own.

In the same way, we should be open if a friend points out that we seem off. Rather than getting defensive, we can listen and see if there is truth in their concern. Good friends want the best for each other, not to shame or control.

---

17. The Value of Consistency

Friendships need some level of consistency to stay strong. That does not mean daily contact or weekly hangouts for everyone, but it does mean not disappearing for months without a word. If you find it hard to keep track, schedule reminders on your phone to check in with important people. That small act can prevent drifting apart.

Some men prefer spontaneous chats, while others like to plan get-togethers a month in advance. Whatever style works, be sure both sides know what to expect. If you have to cancel plans, let your friend know as soon as possible. These polite gestures show you respect their time. Over the long haul, consistent contact builds a deeper sense of connection than sudden bursts of activity followed by silence.

18. Chapter Summary

Building strong friendships can help men feel more connected and supported in everyday life. This chapter covered ways to make new friends, improve existing bonds, and deal with typical problems that can arise. We examined the difference between casual connections and deep relationships, as well as tips for overcoming social fear and awkward starts. We also looked at handling conflict, being a supportive friend, and addressing changes that might happen as life moves on.

The core idea is that friendship requires effort and a willingness to be genuine. Men who show up for each other, listen, keep trust, and respect personal boundaries tend to build closer, long-lasting bonds. Even if life gets busy, consistent small actions—like a phone call or a planned meet-up—can keep a friendship strong. When times get hard, having those connections can make a huge difference in handling sadness or stress.

In the next chapter, we will talk about **setting goals for improvement**. We will look at how men can identify meaningful targets for their mental and physical health, plus methods to stay motivated over the long term. By combining healthy friendships with clear goals, men can move toward a better sense of well-being without feeling alone in the process.

CHAPTER 14: SETTING GOALS FOR IMPROVEMENT

In many areas of life—work, family, personal growth—men often feel a pull to do better. They might sense they are not living up to their potential or that they keep repeating the same mistakes. Setting clear goals can help turn vague wishes into concrete steps, but it is easy to get stuck in daydreams or lose motivation after a few days. This chapter will explain how to set realistic goals, break them down into doable actions, and keep going even when motivation dips. We will also talk about common traps that stop men from reaching their targets, plus ideas on how to adjust goals if life changes in unexpected ways.

Goal-setting is not just about ticking boxes or chasing bigger achievements. It can also boost self-esteem, reduce stress, and give a man a sense of direction. Feeling that you are moving forward, even slowly, can make daily life more meaningful. On the other hand, failing to plan or letting goals remain too abstract can lead to frustration. By learning practical goal-setting skills, men can take ownership of their progress in all parts of life.

---

1. Why Goals Matter for Mental Health

When men struggle with sadness or stress, they might feel stuck in a rut, believing nothing will change. Goals provide structure and a path forward. Achieving even small goals can build confidence, showing that we have some control over our circumstances. Men who set goals often find they develop better habits, like time management, because each day's tasks point toward a bigger aim.

Additionally, goals can act as a buffer against negative thoughts. If you know you are working step by step on a skill, you are less likely to think, "I can't do anything right." Each small win contradicts that harsh idea. Also, goals can help reduce procrastination. Instead of drifting aimlessly, you have a reason to get started each morning.

Goals need not be lofty. They can be as simple as "Walk 15 minutes each day" or "Learn one new recipe every week." The key is making them specific enough that you can measure progress. Instead of saying, "I want to get fit," you might say, "I will follow a basic workout plan twice a week for two months." Clarity and structure matter.

2. The Danger of Vague or Unrealistic Goals

Men sometimes set goals that are too big or too blurry. For example, "I want to be successful" does not tell you which actions to take. Or "I will lose 30 pounds by next month" might be unrealistic and lead to disappointment. When men chase such goals, they might feel crushed if they do not see huge results quickly.

- **Vague goals**: "I want to be happier" or "I want to make more money." Without a plan, these ideas remain wishes.
- **Too large or rushed**: "I need to read 20 books in the next two weeks" is likely not realistic for someone with a full-time job or family duties.
- **No plan for setbacks**: Some men forget to allow room for failure or slow progress. When life throws a curveball, they do not know how to adjust.

Such approaches can bring guilt and a sense of failure. It is better to choose goals that stretch you but are still feasible with consistent effort. That way, you can see progress and stay motivated rather than constantly feeling behind.

3. The SMART Method

One popular technique for setting better goals is called SMART, which stands for:

- **S (Specific)**: The goal is clear and well-defined.
- **M (Measurable)**: You can track progress or success in a concrete way.
- **A (Achievable)**: It is within reach, given your resources and situation.
- **R (Relevant)**: It fits your larger aims in life and your current needs.
- **T (Time-bound)**: There is a set period or deadline.

An example might be: "I will jog for 20 minutes, three times a week, for two months." This states how often, how long, and for how many weeks. It is measurable (time spent running), specific, and you have a deadline (two months). It should also be relevant if your bigger aim is to improve fitness or manage stress through exercise.

Using the SMART format forces you to think more carefully about each part of your plan. Men who skip this step might set random targets that never move them forward. By taking just a few minutes to refine a goal in SMART terms, you raise the chance of actually reaching it.

---

4. Breaking Big Goals into Steps

Sometimes, a man has a big goal, like "Earn a college degree" or "Write a book." At first glance, these can feel huge. Breaking them down into smaller chunks can make them less daunting.

- **Identify the main phases:** For a college degree, you might break it into completing each semester or set of courses. For writing a book, break it into chapters or word counts per week.
- **Make each phase a mini-goal:** "Finish the first chapter by the end of this month," or "Complete 12 credits by the end of the semester."
- **Reward yourself:** After each phase, do something that feels good but does not push you off track. Perhaps watch a favorite movie or cook a nice meal.
- **Evaluate and adjust:** If you finish early, you can move up the timeline. If you miss a step, see why and adapt your plan.

By focusing on one step at a time, you avoid feeling overwhelmed. It is easier to keep going when you see small wins adding up toward the bigger objective.

---

5. Tracking Progress

Keeping track of what you do can make a big difference in staying motivated. This might be a simple notebook, a phone app, or a spreadsheet. Each time you work toward your goal, note how it went. If your goal is to run three days a week, jot down the distance or time. If you plan to read two chapters of a study book daily, mark which chapters you covered.

Seeing a visual record of your steps can build momentum. It reminds you that you are not starting from zero each day. Tracking also helps you notice patterns, like which days you do better or which times you skip tasks. This feedback can inform your next moves. If you see that Tuesday nights are always missed, maybe you can switch the schedule to another time.

Moreover, tracking helps when you feel discouraged. You can look back and realize you have already done more than you thought. This sense of progress can spark the motivation to keep going. Without tracking, it is easy to lose track of how far you have come.

6. Staying Motivated When Enthusiasm Fades

Many men start strong on a new goal but hit a slump after a few weeks. The initial excitement wears off, daily life gets busy, or progress seems slower than expected. Knowing this slump will likely appear can help you prepare:

- **Reconnect with the reason:** Remind yourself why you wanted the goal in the first place. If your goal is to save money, think about how it will help your family or reduce stress.
- **Visual reminders:** Put a note, photo, or chart somewhere you see it daily to reinforce your aim.
- **Check your plan:** Sometimes a dip in motivation means the plan needs adjusting. Maybe you made the steps too hard or too easy.
- **Small rewards:** Aim for small joys after hitting mini-targets. A reward does not have to be expensive. It can be a few minutes doing something you love.
- **Accountability:** Tell a friend about your progress or lack of it. Sharing can push you to stick with the plan instead of quietly giving up.

Most achievements require steady work, not just short bursts. By anticipating the mid-goal slump, men can push through rather than quitting. Overcoming that dip often leads to the real gains in skill and confidence.

7. Handling Setbacks and Failure

No matter how good the plan is, setbacks happen. You might get sick, an unexpected bill might appear, or personal problems might distract you. Men who see setbacks as a reason to quit end up stuck. Instead, think of them as bumps on the road.

1. **Accept the reality:** You lost two weeks of training or had to dip into your savings. It happened.
2. **Reevaluate:** Look at your timetable and see what adjustments are needed. Maybe you extend the deadline or reduce the weekly targets.
3. **Learn from it:** Ask what caused the setback and how you can prepare differently next time. If you got injured from overtraining, you might change your routine to prevent future injuries.
4. **Keep going:** A detour does not mean the goal is gone. Sometimes, you might pause but then resume when ready.

By treating failures as lessons rather than final endings, men can grow stronger. This approach helps build resilience and self-trust. Over time, you become less shaken by unexpected events because you know how to adapt and move forward.

8. Involving Friends or Allies

Goals can be easier and more fun if you do not try to handle them alone. Asking a friend to join you or just to keep you accountable can help maintain momentum. For example:

- **Workout buddies:** Meet at the gym or park at set times. Knowing someone is waiting pushes you to show up.
- **Study partners:** If you have an exam or professional test, pair up with someone else studying. You can test each other on the material.
- **Money-saving circles:** Share monthly savings goals with a close friend. Check each other's progress at the end of the month.
- **Expert mentors:** If your goal is career-related, find someone experienced who can offer tips and watch your growth.

Having a partner can also make the process more social and less stressful. You can share both successes and frustrations, giving each other tips. This mutual support is part of what keeps men going through hard times.

9. Balancing Multiple Goals

Life rarely allows us to focus on just one aim. Men might want to improve health, strengthen relationships, or advance at work all at once. Handling multiple goals requires mindful planning:

- **Set priorities:** Decide which goal is the most urgent or important. That goal might get more time each week.
- **Start small for each goal:** If you want to read more, do not set a massive reading target while also training for a marathon and building a new business. Keep each goal realistic.
- **Use time blocks:** Schedule specific days or times for each aim. For example, Monday, Wednesday, and Friday might be workout days, while Tuesday and Thursday nights are for study or side projects.
- **Watch for overload:** If you find you are constantly stressed or skipping tasks, scale back. Doing fewer goals well is better than doing many goals poorly.

Men sometimes feel they must fix everything at once. But spreading yourself too thin can lead to little progress anywhere. By planning carefully, you can juggle a few goals without burning out.

10. The Power of Deadlines and Timelines

Goals that drag on without an end date often fade. A deadline adds pressure but also provides clarity. You know how long you have to reach a milestone, and you can track each week's progress.

- **Short-term deadlines:** For instance, aim to learn five new words in a foreign language by the end of this week.
- **Mid-term goals:** Maybe set a one- or two-month target, like finishing a certain part of a project.
- **Long-term:** If your overall goal is a year away, break it into smaller check-ins each month or quarter.

Deadlines help men avoid endless procrastination. They also allow for quick corrections if you see you are falling behind. Instead of letting months pass, you can catch problems early and adapt. Just make sure your deadlines are realistic enough to be reached, or else it becomes discouraging.

11. Linking Goals to Personal Values

Sometimes men lose interest in goals because the goals do not match who they are at the core. If your real passion is family time, but you set a goal to work endless overtime hours, your motivation may drop. Aligning goals with values brings deeper satisfaction.

- **Identify core values:** Maybe you value honesty, family, creativity, or helping others.
- **Match goals:** If you value creativity, setting a goal to write or paint each week might give you real joy. If you value health, focusing on a balanced diet and moderate exercise might feel natural.
- **Check conflicts:** If you find your goal clashing with another part of your life, see if you can adjust. For example, if your job goal requires traveling every weekend but you want time with your kids, you might need a different approach.

Men who keep their values in mind often find deeper motivation. It is not just about finishing a task; it is about living a life that fits what truly matters to them.

---

12. Using Visual Boards or Lists

A visual board (sometimes called a vision board) can help keep goals in the front of your mind. It might be a physical poster with images and words cut from magazines, or a digital collage on your phone or computer screen. By looking at it daily, you remind yourself of the outcomes you want. Some men prefer simpler methods, like a checklist on the fridge. The point is to have a tangible reminder that sparks enthusiasm.

- **Images for inspiration:** If your goal is to learn guitar, put pictures of guitars or musicians who inspire you. If you want to improve health, place pictures of healthy meals or an inspiring phrase.
- **Words or phrases:** Include short statements that capture your aims, like "Stronger every day" or "Stay calm in chaos."
- **Update often:** Change or add new pictures as your goals evolve. A static board can become stale after a while.
- **Keep it where you see it:** A closet door, bedroom wall, or phone lock screen. The more you see it, the more it stays in your thoughts.

For men who do not like visual boards, even a simple note on your bathroom mirror listing your three main goals can do the trick. The point is daily reminders.

13. Dealing with Criticism or Lack of Support

Sometimes friends or family might not back your goals. They might say it is not possible, or they might mock the changes you are making. This lack of support can be discouraging. You might also face criticism at work or from strangers on social media if you share your goals publicly.

- **Evaluate feedback:** Sometimes, people have genuine concerns. They might say your timeline is unrealistic or that you are ignoring other duties. If so, consider adjusting.
- **Ignore harmful negativity:** If the feedback is just mocking or jealousy, remind yourself why you started. Seek out people who give constructive responses.
- **Protect your dream:** If you know a certain person always puts you down, avoid discussing your plan with them. Find allies elsewhere.
- **Show results:** Over time, consistent effort can speak for itself. Skeptics might change their tone once they see your progress.

Criticism can sting, but it does not have to end your pursuit. Use it as a test of how badly you want the outcome. In many cases, men find more meaningful connections with new friends who share or support their aims.

---

14. Adjusting Goals as Life Changes

Goals are not set in stone. Life events like a new job, a shift in family duties, or an injury can throw off your original plan. Rather than abandoning the goal entirely, adjust it to the new situation:

- **Change the timeline:** If you planned to complete a project in three months but now have extra responsibilities, stretch it to six months.
- **Reduce or modify steps:** If you cannot train as heavily, focus on gentler exercises. If you cannot study two hours each day, maybe do 30 minutes.
- **Set new priorities:** If a major health issue appears, the top goal might switch to recovery rather than career moves.
- **Keep the spirit:** Even if the details shift, the core aim—like improving your health—can still guide you.

Being flexible shows strength, not weakness. Men who can adapt remain on a forward path even when reality changes. This approach helps protect your mental health from the frustration of impossible demands.

15. Rewards and Celebrations

When men hit a major milestone, it is natural to feel proud. Recognizing progress can boost morale. But be careful that the reward does not undo your hard work. For instance, if your goal was better fitness, a huge binge of unhealthy foods might slow your progress. Instead, pick smaller treats that do not harm the overall effort. (Note: Avoid using the word "celebrate" directly, but you can still talk about rewarding successes.)

- **Healthy treat:** Buy a new book, a new piece of workout gear, or watch a favorite show guilt-free.
- **Social share:** Invite close friends for a casual hangout. Share what you have achieved and have fun talking about the process.
- **Personal break:** If you have been grinding hard, give yourself a day off to rest or do a hobby you enjoy.

Acknowledge that you reached a mini-goal. This moment of recognition can refuel motivation for the next step. Just keep in mind not to go overboard or slip back into old habits.

---

16. Using Failures to Plan Better

If a man falls short of his goal, it can be discouraging. Yet, each failure can be a map showing where the weaknesses are. If you do not lose weight as planned, maybe you realize you snack late at night too often. If you fail an exam, maybe you know you need a study partner or a different learning approach.

- **Collect data:** Look back at what you actually did. Which parts worked? Which days or times were problematic?
- **Brainstorm fixes:** Could you use accountability, change your schedule, or set smaller weekly targets?
- **Stay factual:** Instead of thinking, "I'm just not good enough," examine the facts. Often, the plan or approach had flaws.
- **Try again:** Adjust and do another attempt. Many successful people failed multiple times before they found the right method.

This approach transforms failures into valuable lessons. It teaches resilience. Over time, you learn to see mistakes not as final verdicts but as signposts directing you toward a more effective plan.

17. Keeping Balance and Avoiding Obsession

There is a fine line between being dedicated and being obsessed. If a man becomes so fixated on a goal that he neglects health, relationships, or other duties, it might cause more harm than good. For example, working around the clock might increase income but harm marriage or lead to burnout. Or, chasing extreme physical goals might result in injury or ignoring friends.

- **Check signals:** Are you losing sleep, feeling constant anxiety, or snapping at loved ones? These can be signs you are pushing too hard.
- **Consider a balanced day:** Make sure you leave room for rest, hobbies, and social life, even if your goal is important.
- **Mental health check:** If your stress levels are too high, slow down. Building a better life means being well, not just finishing tasks.

Balance allows for steady growth without crashing. Men who pace themselves often get more done in the long run, because they avoid extreme burnout or emotional distress.

---

18. Chapter Summary

Setting goals is a strong way to lift mood, build self-esteem, and move forward in life. This chapter covered how to avoid vague or unrealistic aims by using the SMART method, breaking large goals into smaller steps, and staying motivated when enthusiasm fades. We also looked at how to handle setbacks, balance multiple goals, and adjust to life's changes. Tracking progress and using small rewards can keep men on course, while seeking help or involving friends can ease loneliness in the process.

The main takeaway is that good goals align with your interests, values, and realistic timelines. They should stretch you but not break you. By planning carefully, taking one step at a time, and learning from mistakes, men can make gradual but steady progress. Each small success gives energy for the next step, helping men see that they do have the power to shape their path.

In upcoming chapters, we will move on to more specifics about treatment options, dealing with setbacks in mental health, and methods to stay motivated. Combining goal-setting with good self-care and social support can bring lasting improvements to a man's mood and outlook, turning everyday life into a place of steady personal growth rather than ongoing worry.

CHAPTER 15: MEDICATION AND OTHER TREATMENTS

Many men who feel sad or low for long periods might consider outside help beyond self-care routines and counseling. Medication and other treatments can play a big part in handling ongoing mood issues. These tools can give relief from severe symptoms and make it easier for a man to work on daily tasks. But it is important to know how these treatments work, what side effects they can have, and how to choose what fits best with personal needs.

In this chapter, we will talk about different types of medications, therapies that use equipment rather than talk, and natural or alternative methods. We will also share key points that may not always be discussed in short articles or casual talks with friends. This chapter is for men who want facts about these choices, so they can discuss them with a doctor or therapist and feel more sure about their decisions.

---

1. Why Men Might Need Medication

Men who face strong sadness might find daily activities nearly impossible. They might be unable to get out of bed, go to work, or care for family duties. Self-help tools and lifestyle changes can help, but sometimes the negative mood is too strong for those methods alone. In these cases, a doctor might propose medication to bring the brain's chemicals closer to a balance that supports better mood and thought processes.

Medications do not turn someone into a different person. Rather, they often give a more stable base to work on other strategies. If a man's mind is overwhelmed by constant gloom or panic, therapy or practical exercises might not sink in. By easing the worst symptoms, medication can open room for other forms of help to do their job.

No one path works for all men. Some may find relief with a certain medication quickly, while others might try several before finding one that fits well. It helps to know that needing medication is not a weakness. It is similar to how a person with high blood pressure might take a pill to keep numbers in a safer range. The main goal is to lessen suffering and allow the mind and body to function more normally.

2. Types of Antidepressants

Many antidepressants fall into a few main groups. Each group works a bit differently on the chemicals in the brain. A doctor or psychiatrist often starts with the safest and best-researched options, then adjusts if the man does not see improvement or has side effects he cannot handle.

1. **SSRIs (Selective Serotonin Reuptake Inhibitors):** Common examples include sertraline, fluoxetine, and citalopram. They increase serotonin levels in the brain by stopping cells from taking too much back in. This can lift mood and reduce anxiety. SSRIs are often the first choice because they tend to have fewer side effects compared to older antidepressants.
2. **SNRIs (Serotonin-Norepinephrine Reuptake Inhibitors):** Examples include venlafaxine and duloxetine. These raise both serotonin and norepinephrine, which can help men with heavy tiredness or physical aches linked to low mood. Some men find SNRIs helpful when SSRIs do not give enough relief.
3. **Bupropion and Others:** Bupropion affects dopamine and norepinephrine instead of serotonin. It can help certain men who experience low energy or who want to avoid some sexual side effects often seen with SSRIs. Another group is older medications called tricyclic antidepressants, which can be effective but may have more side effects.
4. **Atypical Antidepressants:** A few medications do not fit neatly into the above classes. They might target specific chemical patterns in the brain. A psychiatrist might consider them if the common options do not help or cause major problems.

It is best to be open with a doctor about any symptoms, side effects, or concerns. If one medication does not work, switching to another class might make a big difference.

---

3. How Long Medication Takes to Work

Many men expect to feel better a day or two after starting medication, but antidepressants usually need some weeks to show full effects. This waiting period can be frustrating. In the first one or two weeks, some men notice better sleep or a small lift in mood, but the biggest changes often come after four to eight weeks.

It can be tempting to stop a medication if it does not help fast. But giving it enough time is key. If side effects are mild, it is often worth waiting the full trial period suggested by the doctor. However, if side effects are severe, such as intense restlessness or unusual thoughts, contact the doctor right away. There may be a need for a dose change or a shift to a different option.

Many men stay on antidepressants for at least six months to a year once they feel stable. Stopping too soon can cause symptoms to return. A doctor can advise when it is safe to lower the dose or stop fully. Doing this without a plan can bring withdrawal effects, so it is safer to do it under a doctor's guidance.

4. Possible Side Effects of Antidepressants

All medications can have side effects, and it is good to know what might happen before starting treatment. SSRIs, for example, may cause:

- **Upset stomach or diarrhea**
- **Headaches**
- **Sleeping problems** (either feeling too sleepy or having trouble sleeping)
- **Sexual effects**, such as trouble with drive or performance

SNRIs and others can also have side effects, including raised blood pressure, dizziness, or feeling restless. Tricyclic antidepressants might cause dry mouth, constipation, or vision blur. Some men find these side effects manageable, while others feel the medication is not worth it.

Sometimes side effects reduce after a few weeks once the body adjusts. Doctors might suggest taking the medication at a certain time of day, eating a snack with it, or changing the dosage schedule. It is also vital to tell the doctor about any other health conditions or medicines, so they can spot risks like drug interactions. If side effects remain severe, trying a different medication is an option.

5. Medication and Alcohol

Men who take antidepressants should be aware that drinking alcohol can interfere with how well the medication works. In some cases, mixing alcohol with certain medications can increase side effects such as drowsiness or confusion. Also, alcohol itself is a depressant. It can worsen the low mood in the long run, even if it briefly numbs sad feelings.

A small social drink might be fine for some men, but it is wise to talk to a doctor about what is safe. Some men find that staying away from alcohol or limiting it helps the medication do its job more effectively. If drinking is part of a habit to handle sadness, that may be a clue that deeper problems with substance use could be forming.

6. Therapy and Medication Together

Medication can handle chemical imbalances, but talk therapy can show a man how to tackle negative thinking, relationship troubles, or personal habits that feed sadness. Together, these approaches often deliver more stable results. For example, a man might see a counselor every week or two to learn new ways of handling stress. The medication, at the same time, helps him keep a calmer mood so he can practice these lessons in real life.

Cognitive Behavioral Therapy (CBT) is a popular choice, as it focuses on changing the thoughts and actions that keep a person stuck in sadness. Other forms of therapy might look into childhood factors or relationship patterns. Some men attend group therapy for additional support. The point is that combining medication with skill-building can lead to deeper, longer-lasting improvements than either method alone.

7. Other Medical Treatments: TMS and ECT

When men have tried multiple medications and therapies but still feel severe sadness, doctors might propose advanced treatments that use medical equipment. Two well-known methods are TMS (Transcranial Magnetic Stimulation) and ECT (Electroconvulsive Therapy).

- **TMS:** This treatment uses a coil that sends magnetic pulses to specific brain areas involved in mood. It is done while the man is awake in a clinic setting. Each session might last around 20 to 40 minutes, and a man might need daily sessions for a few weeks. Many say they feel only a light

tapping on their head. TMS often helps men who did not respond to several antidepressants.
- **ECT:** This treatment has existed for many years, but it is much safer now than in the past. It uses a quick electrical current to trigger a brief controlled seizure in the brain, under anesthesia. This can help reset brain activity in people with very severe depression or those who have psychotic symptoms. ECT often causes short-term memory issues, but it can bring improvement when other methods have not helped at all.

These methods are usually last-resort steps, but they can be life-changing for men who have tried everything else without relief. Doctors usually discuss them only if multiple rounds of medication have failed or if the man's condition is life-threatening.

---

8. Natural and Alternative Treatments

Some men look for natural or alternative routes instead of mainstream medication. While certain methods might offer mild benefits, it is important to be careful and gather proper facts before choosing them over evidence-based treatments.

- **Herbal supplements (like St. John's Wort):** Some people say these help mood. However, these can interact with other medicines and are not regulated the same way prescription drugs are. A doctor's advice is best before trying them.
- **Omega-3 fatty acids:** Found in fish oil, they may help improve mood balance for some men. They are generally safe when taken properly, but effects are often mild.
- **Light therapy:** Men who live in dark or cold places might use a special light box to mimic sunlight. It is more commonly used for seasonal sadness, but some feel a bit better from this method.
- **Acupuncture or massage:** While not direct cures for deep sadness, these can ease tension and reduce stress. Some men find these approaches good add-ons to other treatments.

If a man uses these methods, it is wise to mention them to his main doctor to avoid possible conflicts with any prescribed medicine or therapy plan.

---

9. Less-Known Options That May Help

1. **Ketamine or Esketamine Treatments:** Ketamine, long used as an anesthetic, in low doses has shown promise in quickly lifting mood in serious cases. An approved form, esketamine, is given as a nasal spray in clinics. It often helps men who have not responded to typical antidepressants. It must be done under supervision due to possible side effects and the need to prevent misuse.
2. **Vagus Nerve Stimulation (VNS):** This involves implanting a small device under the skin of the chest that sends pulses to the vagus nerve in the neck. It can help some men with hard-to-treat sadness. However, this surgery is usually only considered after other methods fail.

These advanced methods are not for mild cases. They show that the medical world is working on new ideas to help severe sadness. If a man has not improved with standard medicines, exploring these options with a psychiatrist might be an option.

---

10. Why Consistent Doctor Visits Are Important

Starting medication is not a one-time event. Doctors usually want to see patients again after a few weeks to check how they are feeling and handle any side effects. Follow-up appointments let men ask questions and report if the medication seems to be working. The doctor can adjust the dose, switch to a new medication, or suggest adding therapy if needed.

For men who find doctor visits annoying, consider that open communication can speed up the time to find the best solution. Without follow-ups, a man might stay on an ineffective dose for too long or quit early, never getting the full benefit. Checking in also helps catch any unexpected problems before they grow worse.

---

11. Dealing with Stigma Around Medication

Many men worry that taking antidepressants will make them seem weak or unable to handle life on their own. Some fear being judged by friends, relatives, or coworkers. But there is no shame in using medical help to fight a serious condition. No one would shame a man for taking insulin if he had diabetes, and this should be no different.

Opening up about medication can be a personal choice. Some men tell close friends or family, while others keep it private. Online support groups can also offer understanding. The important thing is to remember that seeking help is a sign of acting responsibly about health, not a sign of personal failure.

---

12. Therapy Without Medication

It is worth mentioning that not all men need medication. Some experience mild or moderate sadness that can be managed with therapy alone or lifestyle changes. If a man can function at work and home, even if he feels low, therapy might be enough. Tools like CBT, interpersonal therapy, or group counseling might bring improvement without drug side effects.

Signs that therapy alone might be enough include being able to get out of bed, keep up basic tasks, and see small changes when using self-help methods. If a man is unsure, it helps to talk to a mental health expert who can assess the severity. In some cases, a short trial of therapy alone can be tried first, then medication added later if progress stalls.

---

13. Making Lifestyle Changes Alongside Treatment

Men who use medication or other treatments often see bigger benefits if they also maintain good daily habits. These can include:

- **Regular exercise:** Even simple walks or short workouts can help the brain produce mood-friendly chemicals.
- **Balanced diet:** Eating real foods, fruits, vegetables, lean proteins, and whole grains supports general health. Some nutrients also have small but real effects on mood.
- **Proper sleep:** Getting enough rest helps the brain recover. Lack of sleep can hurt mood and worsen negative thoughts.
- **Limiting alcohol and drugs:** Substance use can block progress. Men who want the best results from treatment should address any habits that harm mental health.

Medication alone is not a magic fix. But, added to self-care and therapy, it can speed up positive changes. Committing to a healthier day-to-day routine gives the best chance of feeling better in the short and long run.

14. What to Do if Medication Makes You Feel Flat

A common worry is that antidepressants might remove not just sad feelings but also the ability to feel anything strongly. Some men describe feeling emotionally flat or numb. If this happens, do not just stop taking the medication without advice. Instead, speak to the doctor. A small reduction in dose or a switch to a different class might bring back a normal emotional range while still easing major sadness.

In some cases, men mistake the absence of deep lows for having no feelings at all. It might just take time to get used to a calmer emotional state if they have been weighed down by darkness for a long period. Discussing these feelings with a counselor can help a man understand the changes in his mood and decide if they are too extreme or within a healthy range.

15. Medication for Other Issues Linked to Depression

Men with sadness might also deal with anxiety, panic attacks, or attention problems. In these cases, doctors sometimes add other medications or choose an antidepressant that also helps those conditions. For example, some antidepressants are known to reduce anxiety more than others. If a man struggles with focus, bupropion might help because it can raise alertness.

It is crucial to keep the doctor informed about all symptoms. If a man only talks about low mood, the doctor might miss the anxiety part. A full picture allows the doctor to pick a medication plan that covers as many major symptoms as possible.

16. Keeping an Eye on Warning Signs

In rare cases, antidepressants can raise the risk of harmful thoughts, especially in younger people or early in treatment. A man should let someone he trusts know he has started a new medication. If he feels an increase in dark or harmful thoughts, he should reach out for help right away. This could be contacting a mental health emergency line or calling the doctor to say what is happening.

Though these events are uncommon, it is best to be cautious. Family or friends can watch for changes in a man's behavior, such as withdrawing more than usual, giving away personal items, or making worrying remarks. Quick action can stop a crisis from getting worse.

---

17. Chapter Summary

Medication and other treatments can bring huge relief for men who feel overwhelmed by sadness. Antidepressants adjust brain chemicals to make it easier to manage daily life and learn new coping skills. Other treatments, such as TMS or ECT, can help in cases where several medications have failed. Natural methods may be added for mild support but should be checked with a doctor for safety.

It is important to give medication enough time to work and to have follow-up meetings with the prescribing doctor to handle any side effects or concerns. Using medication is not a sign of weakness; it is a method to address a health issue. In many cases, combining medication with therapy and healthy daily habits offers the best results. If medication is not needed or not helpful, therapy alone might still bring improvement.

In the next chapter, we will look at **handling setbacks**. We will show how to manage times when progress stalls or a man feels he is sliding backward. We will also discuss ways to avoid giving up when sadness returns. By learning how to deal with bumps in the road, men can stay more stable and hopeful during the ups and downs of long-term growth.

CHAPTER 16: HANDLING SETBACKS

Progress in mental health is rarely a straight climb. Men might feel better for weeks, only to have a bad day or a stressful event bring sadness back. These setbacks can cause frustration and self-doubt, especially if a man thought he was already past the worst part of feeling low. But setbacks are normal. They do not cancel out all the progress made so far. This chapter focuses on how to react in these tough moments, so men do not lose hope or quit helpful routines.

We will talk about normal triggers for setbacks, such as stress at work, family problems, or changes in sleep and habits. We will also cover ways to see warning signs early, plus methods to bounce back as quickly as possible. By understanding that setbacks are part of the process, men can learn to face them with fewer feelings of shame or panic.

---

1. Why Setbacks Happen

A setback might mean a week of feeling sad after a period of feeling better. Or it might be a burst of anger or anxiety that catches a man by surprise. These moments often happen due to shifts in daily life. For example, a breakup or job loss can spark waves of sadness. Even good events, like moving to a bigger house, can bring stress that makes mood issues flare.

Sometimes setbacks happen for no clear reason. The brain can be influenced by subtle hormonal or seasonal changes. A man might also forget to keep up with habits that were helping, like regular exercise or social contact. Over time, old patterns of negative thinking can sneak back if not watched.

Setbacks do not mean all progress has vanished. They show that mood problems can remain sensitive, and constant maintenance is needed. Recognizing this helps men stay alert and be ready to use the tools they learned to stay on track.

---

2. Spotting Warning Signs Early

One key way to handle setbacks is to see them coming. If a man notices he is getting more irritable, or his sleep is off, that can be a sign that stress is building. Other red flags might include skipping meals or workouts, ignoring calls from friends, or suddenly drinking more alcohol.

By keeping an eye on mood and behavior changes, a man can step in before a small slip becomes a major fall. This could mean scheduling a therapy appointment if negative thoughts grow stronger, or reaching out to a friend if loneliness is rising. Writing mood notes each day, even just a number from 1 to 10, can reveal small declines quickly.

Catching these signs can be tough, especially if old habits lean toward denial. But men who push past the urge to ignore problems often find they can reverse a slump faster by acting right away.

3. The Mindset for Handling Bad Days

When men have a really bad day, they might think, "Here we go again. I'm right back at the start." But a single bad day does not wipe out months of growth. Trying to see it as just a temporary dip can reduce hopelessness. A helpful thought might be, "I'm having a rough time right now, but this feeling has passed before, and I can do my best to manage it again."

Reminding yourself of previous successes can bring perspective. Think about how you got through a similar slump in the past. Maybe you used breathing exercises, took a break from extra obligations, or talked to a friend. That means you have evidence of your ability to cope. The more a man sees a setback as a short detour rather than a failure, the calmer he can stay.

4. Practical Steps to Use When You Feel a Dip

1. **Pause and reflect:** Ask yourself what might be causing the change in mood or energy. Did something stressful occur? Have you stopped some helpful habit like daily walks?
2. **Check your basic needs:** Make sure you are eating well, drinking enough water, and getting enough sleep. These small factors can have a big effect.
3. **Talk to someone:** This could be a counselor, friend, or family member. Saying how you feel often helps reduce the weight, and they might see solutions you do not.
4. **Review your coping list:** If you have written down tools for stress (breathing drills, going for a run, writing in a journal), pick one and do it. Even if you feel unmotivated, taking one action can nudge you in a better direction.

These steps are like first aid for a low mood. They may not fix everything, but they can keep a bad day from turning into a much deeper crisis.

5. Handling Self-Criticism and Blame

When men hit setbacks, they might become harsh on themselves, saying, "I should be stronger," or "I must have messed up." This blame can deepen the slump by adding guilt to sadness. Recognizing this inner critic is important, as we mentioned in previous chapters.

To lower self-blame, it helps to remember that mood issues are not just about willpower. Even with good efforts, the brain can slip back into low states, especially if faced with stress. Replacing "I failed" with "I'm facing a tough moment, but I'm still learning" can shift the mindset. Try to speak to yourself in a supportive tone, like you would to a friend going through a hard time.

6. Checking If You Slipped on Self-Care

Men often drop self-care when they feel better, thinking they no longer need it. They might stop seeing a therapist or quit journaling because they believe the problem has passed. Then, if a sudden stress hits, they do not have the same defenses in place. This can lead to a stronger setback.

A quick check might involve asking: "Am I still doing the things that helped me climb out of sadness before?" If the answer is no, it is a sign to restart them. This does not always fix the slump right away, but it lays a foundation to keep the low mood from getting worse.

7. Revisiting Professional Help

Even if you felt progress after counseling or medication, a big setback might call for professional input again. Therapy might not need to last for many months. Sometimes just a few sessions can refresh your coping skills. Or if you are on medication, you might need a dose adjustment or a different prescription if the current one has lost some of its effect.

There is no shame in going back to a doctor or therapist after a break. Life changes, and so do the demands on the mind. A relationship that was stable before might end, or a new job could raise stress levels. Each shift can change what a man needs to stay mentally balanced. Staying open to more help when needed is a sign of being proactive, not weak.

8. Turning Setbacks into Learning Points

One lesser-known approach is to treat each setback as a clue. A man can ask, "What can I learn about my triggers or coping style from this event?" If a family argument led to a bad slump, maybe that shows how important clear boundaries at home are. If working 70 hours a week led to burnout, it might show that strict limits on overtime are needed.

Making notes on each setback can reveal patterns. Over time, a man might see that certain months or situations always bring low mood. Knowing this, he can plan ahead—maybe schedule counseling sessions or lighten his workload during that period. This planning can reduce the size and length of future setbacks.

9. Safety Plan for Severe Slumps

Men who experience very low points might worry about harmful thoughts. A safety plan is a written list of steps to take if these thoughts appear. It can include:

- **Warning signs**: List the thoughts, feelings, or actions that show a major slump is near.
- **Coping methods**: Write down immediate actions like calling a friend, doing a short exercise, or changing the environment.
- **Contacts**: Include phone numbers of trusted friends, family, or crisis lines.
- **Professional support**: Have the number of your therapist, doctor, or local mental health center ready.

Keeping this list in a phone or a wallet means it is always on hand. It helps reduce panic by giving clear steps. Even if a man never needs the plan, having it can bring peace of mind that he is prepared.

10. Sharing About Setbacks with Others

Many men try to keep setbacks private, worried they will be seen as weak or unreliable. But telling at least one trusted person can relieve some pressure. A friend might say, "I understand, I've been there," or offer a helping hand with chores while you rest. A romantic partner might adjust plans or simply give emotional support.

Hiding a slump often makes it feel bigger, as the man might fear being found out. Openness does not mean sharing details with everyone. But picking a person who can offer empathy can lighten the load. Also, hearing an outside view might show that the setback is not as large as it feels inside one's own head.

---

11. Re-building Routines

When a slump disrupts daily life, returning to a steady routine can help. This routine might include:

- **Set sleep times**: Going to bed and waking up at the same hour supports more stable energy levels.
- **Regular meals**: Skipping meals or eating junk food can worsen mood swings.
- **Planned activities**: Even if you do not feel like doing much, having a short walk or a small task in your plan can keep momentum.
- **Social check-ins**: Schedule small calls or texts to stay connected, rather than withdrawing fully.

Rebuilding these basics can be hard at first if a man feels no motivation. But pushing through a lack of desire can be important. Each completed part of the routine is a small success that can start shifting the mood upward again.

---

12. Using Breaks Wisely

Sometimes a man needs a break from certain stresses when a setback occurs. This might be a short break from a tough project at work, or a day off to handle personal issues. If anxiety is sky-high, stepping back can prevent a worse crash. But it is important not to use breaks as a way to avoid all responsibilities forever.

Taking a break can also mean doing something calming for a set period: a walk outside, listening to music, or writing in a journal. The aim is to reduce mental overload, then return to tasks with a slightly clearer head. Some men find that short breaks each day prevent stress from building to a crisis.

13. Avoiding the "All or Nothing" Trap

A big pitfall during setbacks is thinking in extremes. A man might say, "Because I missed two days of exercise, I might as well give up on fitness completely." Or "I snapped at my partner, so I am a terrible person." These thoughts ignore the middle ground, which is where real life usually happens.

By avoiding these black-and-white views, a man can see that a small slip does not erase all progress. Missing a couple of workouts does not mean healthy living is doomed. Apologizing for snapping and then doing better next time can repair the moment. Staying open to partial success can protect mood and keep hope alive, even when not everything goes perfectly.

14. Adjusting Goals and Expectations

Setbacks might show that old goals need tweaking. If a man set a goal to run 5 miles every morning but got injured, he might need to lower it to 2 miles or switch to walking. If a big project deadline is causing sleepless nights, he might ask for an extension or share tasks with a colleague.

Resisting these adjustments can create unneeded strain. Being flexible ensures that a short-term slump does not turn into a bigger problem. It does not mean quitting goals—it means fitting them to current reality. Later, when the slump eases, the man can push forward again.

15. Looking for Hidden Triggers

Sometimes the cause of a setback is not obvious. A man might think everything is fine, but inside he might be angry about something or worried about an upcoming event. Writing or talking can help uncover these hidden triggers.

Maybe an approaching holiday stirs up painful memories. Or a coworker's comments bring back shame from the past.

Once found, these triggers can be addressed more directly. For instance, if family gatherings cause tension, a man can plan coping methods or reduce how much time he spends there. If money stress is the hidden trigger, making a budget or contacting a financial advisor can lower anxiety. Identifying triggers is half the battle in preventing a slump from taking over.

---

16. Positive Self-Talk During a Setback

Self-talk has a big effect on how men handle difficulties. During a slump, negative thoughts might dominate: "I'm worthless," "I can't deal with anything." But a man can practice short, realistic statements that remind him setbacks are temporary.

- "I've overcome bad days before; I can do it again."
- "This feeling is tough, but it will not last forever."
- "I deserve to treat myself with patience right now."

These statements might feel fake at first, especially if gloom is heavy. But repeating them can anchor the mind away from total despair. They are not magic words, but they can keep a man from sinking further into negative thinking.

---

17. Knowing When to Seek Immediate Help

Sometimes a slump is more than just a rough patch. If a man has harmful thoughts toward himself or others, hears voices, or cannot manage basic tasks like eating or washing, professional help should be sought quickly. This might mean contacting a mental health helpline, going to a hospital, or calling a trusted person who can assist.

Immediate help can be the difference between life and death in extreme cases. There is no shame in needing crisis support. Many men fear being judged, but crisis hotlines and emergency rooms are used to helping people in mental health emergencies. Acting quickly is always better than hoping the thoughts will vanish on their own.

18. Chapter Summary

Setbacks are a natural part of recovering from sadness or other mood problems. They do not mean a man has lost all his progress. Instead, they show that mental health requires ongoing care. By noticing warning signs, using coping steps right away, and being kind to themselves, men can lower the impact of these slumps.

Practical actions—like reviewing self-care routines, talking openly, and adjusting goals—can shorten the length and depth of setbacks. In more serious cases, returning to therapy or professional help might be needed. Each slump can offer lessons about triggers, boundaries, and best practices for staying balanced.

In the chapters to come, we will share ideas for staying motivated for change, talking openly about personal struggles, and finding resources for ongoing support. By understanding how to handle setbacks, men can move forward with less fear. They will know that an occasional stumble does not mean they must give up. With patience and the right steps, better days can return, and each challenge can add new insights for long-term stability.

CHAPTER 17: STAYING MOTIVATED FOR CHANGE

Staying motivated can be a big challenge for men trying to handle sadness or stress. It is normal to feel excited when you first begin to make changes, only to lose energy later. You might stick with new habits for a short time, then slip back into older, unhelpful routines. This can happen whether you are working on improving your mood, changing your diet, or creating better boundaries at work.

In this chapter, we will talk in detail about why motivation often comes and goes, and how to keep some spark alive even when stress levels rise. We will explore real steps men can take, such as finding supportive people or setting practical short-term targets. We will also address hidden factors, like self-criticism and external pressures, that can kill motivation. By understanding these issues, a man can stand a better chance of moving steadily toward better mental health, rather than jumping in and out of progress.

---

1. Why Motivation Fades Over Time

Many men feel a burst of energy when they decide to improve their lives. For example, a man might tell himself, "I'm finally going to get into shape," or "I will talk to a therapist and feel better fast." This boost can last days or weeks, but then daily problems pop up—busy work schedules, family duties, or simple tiredness. When faced with these real-life obstacles, the original spark can fizzle out.

Reasons motivation fades:

1. **Unrealistic expectations:** If a man expects quick results, any delay can make him think his efforts are useless.
2. **Lack of visible progress:** Men might lose drive if they do not see clear benefits early on, such as improved mood or better energy.
3. **Everyday stressors:** Bills, child care, and job tasks can take priority, pushing self-care to the side.
4. **Isolation:** Without a friend or group to lean on, a man might feel alone in his changes, which can make it easy to quit.

Understanding that motivation usually dips after the initial excitement helps men plan ahead. Knowing that it is not about personal weakness but about normal human patterns can reduce shame. There is no need to label yourself as lazy if your spark drops. Instead, focus on methods to handle that dip before it pulls you away from positive steps.

---

2. Setting Clear and Personal Reasons

Motivation often holds better when it is linked to meaningful reasons. A vague goal such as "I should be healthier" might not keep you going when you are tired and stressed. In contrast, "I want to have enough energy to play with my kids after work" is a clear, personal reason.

Ways to define personal reasons:

- **Ask deeper questions:** Why do you want to improve your mood or shape? It might be for family, confidence, or to reduce daily pain.
- **Write it down:** Put your reasons in a place you see daily, like on your phone or a note in your wallet.
- **Review often:** Reread those reasons when you do not feel like exercising or when you think about skipping therapy sessions.

When the push to give up appears, seeing a reminder of what truly matters can reignite the will to continue. Personal reasons anchor your decisions in meaningful values rather than external pressure.

---

3. Creating an Environment That Supports You

Environment plays a big role in motivation. If you are surrounded by triggers that pull you back into old habits, you will have to fight an uphill battle every day. On the other hand, an environment set up for success can reduce friction.

Steps to shape your environment:

1. **Remove temptations:** If you are trying to cut back on alcohol, do not keep bottles in the house. If you want better sleep, move the TV or phone away from your bedside at night.
2. **Organize helpful tools:** Keep a yoga mat, weights, or exercise shoes in a visible spot if you plan to work out regularly. If journaling helps your mood, keep a notebook within reach.

3. **Use reminders:** Alarms on your phone can prompt you to take breaks, do short breathing drills, or plan your meals. Sticky notes on the mirror or fridge can push you to stick with new habits.
4. **Seek supportive people:** Spend more time with friends who encourage your progress. If certain individuals constantly mock your efforts, limit your contact with them when possible.

Sometimes men think strong willpower should beat a bad environment. But it is more practical to reduce obstacles, so you do not have to rely on willpower alone. Adjusting your space and social surroundings makes it easier to keep going when the initial burst of motivation decreases.

---

4. Breaking Big Steps into Smaller Actions

If you aim to do something large—like overhaul your eating habits, tackle emotional baggage, or train for a serious athletic event—this can be intimidating. At first, that intimidation might push you to try too much too soon. Then, frustration sets in when real life gets in the way.

How to break bigger goals down:

- **Pick micro-goals:** Instead of aiming to run 5 miles right away, start with a 10-minute jog. Instead of planning a complete diet change, begin by adding an extra serving of vegetables to lunch.
- **Track mini-progress:** Mark a calendar each time you meet a small target. This can give a sense of success and keep momentum.
- **Adjust as you go:** Once a small step feels easy, move up to something slightly harder. Gradual increases can build confidence and reduce the chance of injury or burnout.

When men see themselves achieving a small step each day, they start to believe they can handle the next level. This repeated success can re-ignite motivation whenever it dips.

---

5. Leveraging Accountability

Accountability means letting someone else know about your goals, so they can check on you. This might feel awkward for men who are used to handling their problems alone, but it can be a huge boost. Knowing someone will ask how you are doing can keep you from quitting at the first sign of trouble.

Practical accountability methods:

1. **Buddy system:** Find a coworker, friend, or online contact with a similar goal. Check in daily or weekly.
2. **Public declarations:** Announce a plan to a group, like a social media post: "I will be working out three times a week." The thought of letting others down can push you to keep going.
3. **Regular check-ups:** This could be with a therapist, doctor, or support group. Scheduled meetings force you to review progress and be honest about struggles.

When men try to do everything in silence, it is easier to quit because no one else sees. Accountability does not have to mean oversharing. Even a small circle of trusted people can help keep the fire burning when you feel lazy or discouraged.

---

6. Using Rewards and Healthy Treats

Rewarding yourself is a normal way to maintain motivation. However, it is important to pick rewards that do not sabotage your progress. For instance, using junk food as a reward might conflict with weight or health targets.

Examples of positive rewards:

- **Personal time:** After a week of following your plan, spend an hour doing something you love, like reading a favorite book or playing a game.
- **Minor purchases:** Buy a new shirt or tool if it is within your budget, and only if it does not conflict with any financial goals.
- **Experience-based treats:** Go to a small local event or watch a sports match with a friend. Shared activities can reinforce social ties as well.

By giving yourself something positive to look forward to, you add a sense of fun to the work of self-improvement. Rewards also help your mind link consistent effort with a feeling of success, making you more likely to stay on track.

---

7. Handling Plateaus and Boredom

When trying to improve mental health or physical wellness, it is normal to hit a plateau—a period where it seems you are not moving forward. Men might feel bored doing the same routines. The mood might not show more improvement, or the body stops changing. This lull can tempt a man to give up.

Ways to tackle plateaus:

1. **Change the approach:** If your exercise routine is stale, try a new activity. If therapy feels repetitive, consider asking your counselor to focus on different topics or methods.
2. **Look for small signs of progress:** Mood changes might be subtle, like less anger in the morning or better sleep. These tiny wins mean you are still improving.
3. **Adjust goals:** If you reached a certain level, set a new one that challenges you but is still realistic.
4. **Reflect on habits:** Plateaus sometimes reveal that the old plan is no longer enough. You might need an extra push or a fresher approach.

Plateaus are not proof of failure. They are part of the natural cycle of growth. Men who accept them as normal can try creative ways to spark new energy rather than walking away.

---

8. Knowing When to Pause or Slow Down

Sometimes men push themselves too hard, either to prove something or out of fear of losing momentum. This can lead to burnout. If you feel exhausted all the time or your relationships are suffering because you spend all your energy on self-improvement tasks, it could be time to ease off.

Signs you might need a short break or a slower pace:

- Chronic fatigue that does not improve with sleep
- Frequent irritability with family or friends
- Physical aches or stress-related pains that keep getting worse
- Feeling mentally numb or disconnected

Pausing does not mean quitting. It can be a planned rest—like taking a few days off from intense exercise or scheduling fewer therapy sessions for a short period. Make sure the pause is intentional and has a plan for returning. This can give the mind and body space to recover, so motivation can regrow.

9. Renewing Motivation Through New Sources

If you feel stuck, seeking new sources of information or inspiration can give a second wind. Men often find fresh insights from talking to others who have faced similar struggles. Reading books or articles can spark new ideas. Online forums or support groups might open your eyes to strategies you never tried.

Ideas for new motivation boosts:

- **Podcasts or videos:** Listen to mental health podcasts while commuting, or watch short clips that teach stress management.
- **Local classes or workshops:** Attend a short course on a topic like mindfulness, healthy cooking, or a hobby you have never explored.
- **Mentoring or volunteering:** Helping someone else can also refresh your own sense of purpose. Teaching another person a skill can remind you why you valued it in the first place.

Staying in a bubble can lead to stale routines. Getting new input can show you simpler ways to keep going or remind you that you are not alone in your efforts.

10. Dealing with Negative Opinions from Others

Sometimes men try to make changes, only to get negative remarks from those around them. A coworker might tease you for eating healthier. A friend might brush off your plan to reduce drinking. Family members could be skeptical, saying, "You've tried that before." These reactions can hurt motivation, especially if you crave acceptance.

How to handle negative feedback:

1. **Stay calm and firm:** Try a polite response like, "I'm doing this for my own reasons, and it's important to me."
2. **Limit details:** You do not have to explain everything. A brief explanation or none at all can avoid a drawn-out debate.

3. **Seek better support:** Spend time with people who back your goals, even if they are just online contacts.
4. **Turn negativity into resolve:** Some men use skepticism as fuel to prove doubters wrong. However, make sure your main motivation stays personal, not just about proving a point.

You cannot control how others respond, but you can decide how to react. If the remarks are mild teasing, brush them off. If they are truly harmful, setting limits on that relationship might be needed. The more you stand by your decision, the easier it gets to ignore outside voices.

11. Tracking and Reviewing Achievements

A solid way to stay motivated is to have a record of your achievements. This goes beyond mental notes. You might keep a log of workouts done, pages read, therapy sessions attended, or mood improvements. Even small notations of daily successes can remind you of how far you have come.

How to track improvements:

- **Simple daily log:** A notebook where you record if you stuck to your plan (like "Walked 20 minutes today, ate balanced meals").
- **Occasional self-check:** Every week, write a few sentences about what went right, what was hard, and what you learned.
- **Visual charts or apps:** Some apps let you track mood or tasks completed. Seeing a streak of accomplishments often makes you want to keep it up.

When you feel your motivation wane, reviewing these logs can remind you that progress is real. It might also give clues as to why motivation dipped—maybe you see that each time you skip journaling, you lose some sense of direction.

12. Balancing Self-Compassion with Self-Discipline

Some men swing between extreme self-criticism and letting themselves off the hook for everything. Both extremes can harm motivation. True self-compassion means being kind when mistakes happen, but also holding yourself accountable to keep aiming for progress.

- **What is healthy discipline?** It means sticking to routines even when not in the mood, but without punishing yourself if you slip. For instance, if you miss one workout, you get back on track the next day instead of giving up or being harsh on yourself.
- **What is self-compassion?** Recognizing that everyone makes mistakes or has bad days, and speaking to yourself in a supportive way. Instead of, "I'm useless," say, "I had a tough day, but I'll try again tomorrow."

By combining these two approaches, men can remain motivated without pushing themselves into shame or burnout. It is a middle path that promotes consistent effort along with understanding that we are all human.

---

13. Updating Goals to Match Your Growth

As you keep working on mental health, older goals might no longer fit. Maybe you started with the aim to reduce panic attacks, but now you rarely have them. This is a success, and it might be time to set a new challenge—like improving social confidence or learning a new skill that was too scary before.

Signs it is time to update goals:

- You have reached a major milestone and feel stable.
- The daily tasks are too easy and no longer excite you.
- Your interests have shifted due to new experiences or insights.
- You want to explore deeper topics in therapy or new physical challenges.

Goals are not static. Adjusting them keeps your motivation alive because you always have something meaningful to aim for. Otherwise, you might end up coasting, which can eventually lead to boredom or loss of direction.

---

14. Recognizing the Long-Term View

Improving mental health or building new habits is not something that ends in a few weeks. It often takes months or even years to establish strong, lasting change. Recognizing this bigger timeline can prevent you from panicking if results are slow.

How to keep a long-term mindset:

1. **Think in phases:** Maybe focus on simple self-care (sleep, basic exercise) for the first month, then add therapy or group activities in the second month, and so on.
2. **Value incremental gains:** Even a 5% improvement in mood or stamina is progress. Over many months, those small gains stack up.
3. **Accept occasional setbacks:** As we covered previously, a slump does not mean your entire plan fails. Stay the course.
4. **Plan for maintenance:** Once you reach a stable point, think about how to keep it. That might mean fewer therapy sessions but still a monthly check-in. Or a reduced exercise schedule but one that is consistent.

By seeing your efforts as part of a longer path, you avoid the trap of feeling like you failed if you are not perfect right away. Real mental health improvements can be slow, but they are more solid when built step by step.

---

15. Mental Exercises to Boost Inner Drive

Sometimes men lose motivation because they get stuck in negative self-talk or looped thinking. Specific mental exercises can help refocus on what you are doing well and what you want to achieve.

- **Brief visualization:** Imagine yourself doing the habit you want (like calmly talking to a partner instead of blowing up, or completing a workout). Picture the details—the place, how you feel, the steps you take. This can prepare the mind to accept that this behavior is possible.
- **Positive note-taking:** Write down one good action you took each day related to your goals. Keep this note visible.
- **Countering negativity:** When your brain says, "I can't keep this up," reply with a factual statement like, "I managed it three times last week, so I can do it again."

Such exercises might seem small, but they change the mental environment. Over time, they reduce the power of negative thoughts and strengthen the belief that progress is possible.

---

16. Asking for Help When You Slip

Sometimes the best move is to directly ask someone for help in re-finding your motivation. This might be a mental health professional, a mentor, a friend who succeeded in a similar area, or even a family member who is known for being positive. Men often resist asking because they worry it will look weak. In truth, most people understand how tough it can be to stay on track.

Reaching out can take many forms:

- A simple text: "I'm struggling to keep up with my plan. Can we talk?"
- A scheduled call: Ask a friend to call once a week for the next month to see how you are doing.
- A short meeting with a therapist: Even if you had therapy in the past, going back for a "tune-up" session can spark new ideas.

Letting someone into your process can not only bring fresh motivation, but it can also uncover hidden barriers you did not notice. They may offer solutions that never occurred to you, or just the presence of another person can help you push forward.

---

17. Avoiding Perfectionism

Perfectionism is a common trap for men wanting to improve. They might demand they stick to their plan with 100% accuracy or see major changes every week. When reality does not match these expectations, they get angry or disappointed. This can kill motivation quickly.

Strategies to let go of perfectionism:

- **Set realistic success markers:** For instance, if you want to exercise five days a week, accept that missing one day does not ruin the entire week.
- **Recognize partial success:** Doing 20 minutes of a planned 30-minute workout is still helpful. Having a quick chat with a counselor instead of a full session can still make a difference.
- **View mistakes as data:** Instead of saying, "I messed everything up," ask, "What can I learn from this event?"
- **Celebrate small steps:** Even if you only improved a little, that counts.

By lowering the need for everything to be perfect, you remove a huge layer of stress. That stress, when gone, frees up energy for consistent progress.

18. Chapter Summary

Motivation is not a permanent thing that men either have or do not have. It often starts strong, fades under real-life pressures, and must be nurtured and renewed over time. Keeping your motivation alive involves building an environment that supports your goals, breaking big aims into smaller steps, and rewarding yourself with healthy treats. Accountability—whether from friends, mentors, or online groups—can help you keep going when you feel like quitting.

Additionally, learning to handle setbacks, plateaus, and boredom is crucial. Men who accept that progress takes months or years, rather than days, tend to stay patient with themselves. Self-compassion helps avoid harsh self-talk, while consistent effort—backed by a realistic plan—prevents burnout. When negativity or perfectionism creeps in, small mental exercises or short breaks can get you back on course. Finally, if motivation truly plummets, seeking help from professionals or trusted allies can reignite the drive to change.

Staying motivated is about more than sheer willpower. It is about shaping a life context—friends, routines, spaces, and thoughts—that makes it simpler to keep making healthy choices. In the next chapter, **SHARING YOUR STORY**, we will talk about how opening up can connect men to others in meaningful ways, reduce shame, and possibly inspire people around you to get help if they need it too.

CHAPTER 18: SHARING YOUR STORY

Talking about personal struggles with sadness can feel risky. Men often grow up hearing that they should handle their problems alone. Many worry that revealing low mood or anxiety might lead to judgment or pity. Yet, sharing your story—whether in a small circle of friends, online forums, or larger speaking events—can bring real benefits. It can heal old wounds and show other men that they are not alone in feeling this way.

In this chapter, we will talk about the positives and potential pitfalls of sharing personal experiences with sadness. We will cover methods to choose the right audience, set limits on how much to reveal, and prepare for different reactions. We will also look at how some men decide to go public with their stories to help others see that seeking help is not a sign of weakness. By learning to speak about personal trials in a safe, honest way, a man can lighten his own load while possibly guiding someone else toward hope.

---

1. Why Telling Personal Stories Matters

When men share the reality of feeling low or having a hard time, it challenges the idea that only "weak" people struggle. It helps break down stigma by showing that sadness can happen to anyone, including individuals who appear successful or strong on the outside. This allows other men—who might be suffering in silence—to see they are not odd or alone. Hearing, "I went through that too," can be a relief and a reason for them to open up.

Key benefits of speaking out:

1. **Personal relief:** Putting tough feelings into words can release some of the tension you have been holding.
2. **Connection with others:** Sharing encourages mutual support. A friend or stranger might respond, "I've felt that way as well," forming an instant bond.
3. **Encouraging change:** Sometimes, men who speak about their experiences learn about new resources, like better therapists or supportive events, from listeners who want to help.
4. **Inspiring others:** Your story might prompt a friend to seek counseling or talk to a doctor, changing their life path for the better.

Of course, sharing does not mean you must reveal every detail of your past or every deep thought. Men should find a level of openness that feels right and safe for them.

---

2. Deciding What and How Much to Share

Every man has a different comfort zone for personal information. Some might only feel safe talking about surface issues—like "I've been feeling low for a while." Others might be ready to describe childhood events or major traumas. The point is to choose what fits your current state. Oversharing can lead to regret, but undersharing might keep you feeling isolated.

Questions to ask before sharing:

- **Who is my audience?** Are you talking to a single close friend, a group of coworkers, or an online forum? Each setting might require a different level of detail.
- **What do I hope to gain?** Is it to get advice, to educate others, or just to feel less alone? Being clear on your goal can guide how much you say.
- **How might this affect me emotionally?** Telling certain stories might bring up painful memories. Make sure you are prepared to handle any emotional rush.
- **Is this the right time and place?** Sharing serious issues at a loud party might not be effective. A quiet moment with someone who cares is usually better.

You do not owe everyone an explanation of your feelings. It is okay to be selective. Some men start with short mentions of sadness and see how the listener reacts before going deeper. That approach can help you judge if the person or group is likely to be supportive.

---

3. Practicing Openness with Trusted People

If you have never spoken about your sadness out loud, it can feel odd. Practicing with one person you trust—maybe a close friend or family member—can help you find the words. You might feel shaky at first, or worry you sound weak or silly. Remember that talking about emotions is a skill that grows with practice.

Steps for a practice talk:

1. **Choose a calm moment:** Let the person know you want to share something important. Ask if they have time to listen without rush.
2. **State your feelings simply:** You might say, "I've been feeling really down for the past few months. It's been affecting my sleep and how I handle stress."
3. **Explain what you want from them:** Are you looking for advice, a listening ear, or help finding a counselor? Make it clear, so they know how to respond.
4. **Watch their reaction:** A caring listener might show empathy, ask questions, or just let you speak. If you sense negative or dismissive vibes, it might not be the right person to open up to.

Over time, such practice helps you speak more naturally about your internal world. It can also reveal who in your life can truly handle deep topics.

---

4. Potential Risks of Sharing

While sharing can be healing, it is not always simple. Some men might face confusion or negative judgment from people who do not understand mental health issues. Coworkers might see you differently if you openly talk about sadness in a professional setting. Family members could blame you or tell you to "toughen up." These reactions can hurt.

Common risks:

- **Feeling vulnerable or exposed:** Once you share, you cannot completely undo that knowledge in the other person's mind.
- **Receiving poor advice or harsh remarks:** Well-meaning people might offer unhelpful tips like "Just be positive." Others might mock or belittle the problem.
- **Social or professional impact:** In some work cultures, men fear losing respect if they admit to emotional struggles.
- **Emotional overload:** Talking about painful events can bring up strong feelings. If you do not have coping strategies, it might be overwhelming.

To reduce these risks, choose your audience carefully. Start with people known for being open-minded or with professionals trained to handle such conversations. If negative reactions happen, remember that it says more about their lack of understanding than about your worth.

5. Sharing in Support Groups or Therapy Circles

Support groups can be a halfway point between private talks and public sharing. Such groups often have rules about confidentiality, so what is said in the group stays there. Men can talk about personal experiences without worrying it will spread to their workplace or extended family.

Benefits of a group setting:

1. **Common ground:** Everyone is there for similar reasons, whether it is depression, anxiety, or coping with a loss.
2. **Peer feedback:** Hearing how other men overcame certain obstacles can spark new ideas for your own life.
3. **Regular meetings:** Consistent sessions help track your mood and keep you open, rather than bottling things up for months.
4. **Less isolation:** You see firsthand that you are not the only one dealing with deep sadness or stress.

Group therapy or community support meetings can be found through local mental health centers, churches, or online directories. If speaking in front of a small group feels too scary at first, you can attend and just listen until you feel ready to share.

---

6. Using Online Platforms Carefully

Online forums and social media can be a double-edged sword. On one hand, you can find communities of men who relate to your story. Anonymity might allow you to open up more. On the other hand, trolls or insensitive comments can do damage. Also, once something is online, you might not control who sees it.

Tips for online sharing:

- **Choose the right platform:** There are mental health forums where moderation is stricter, reducing bullying or harsh remarks.
- **Protect personal details:** If you prefer anonymity, do not reveal your full name, exact location, or work details.
- **Read for a while first:** Observe how people react to posts. This shows whether it is a supportive place or filled with mean behavior.
- **Know your limits:** If a conversation turns heated or negative, step away rather than letting it cause more stress.

Some men find significant support and long-term friends through online groups. Others find it best to use them only as a first step before seeking face-to-face connections. Keep in mind that online interactions cannot always replace real-life relationships, especially in times of crisis.

---

7. Sharing for Advocacy or Public Awareness

Some men decide to speak about their experiences in a bigger way—such as writing blog posts, giving talks, or creating social media content. This can help fight the stigma around mental health by making the topic more visible. However, going public also exposes you to a larger audience, which might include critics or strangers who misjudge you.

Reasons men choose public advocacy:

1. **Desire to help others:** They might want to show that it is normal to seek treatment.
2. **Creating social change:** Speaking openly can push workplaces or communities to offer better mental health support.
3. **Personal healing:** Telling your story in a structured way can sometimes boost self-confidence and reduce the shame men feel about past issues.

However, public sharing requires planning. Think about whether you want to share certain personal details. Prepare for a range of reactions—most might be kind, but a few could be critical. It helps to have a support system in place for yourself if negative feedback arises.

---

8. Handling Emotional Responses While Sharing

It is possible to become emotional or tearful when talking about deeper topics, especially if the memories still carry pain. For men who grew up believing they must hide tears, this can feel embarrassing. Yet, showing honest emotion can help others see the realness of your feelings.

Steps to handle emotions while talking:

1. **Pause when needed:** If tears come, take a moment to breathe. A short pause is okay.

2. **Give yourself an out:** If you are talking in a group, let them know you might stop if it gets too heavy. People usually understand.
3. **Stay hydrated and calm:** Sipping water or focusing on slow breathing can ground you if your heartbeat speeds up.
4. **Plan a self-care step afterward:** This could be listening to calming music, taking a walk, or calling a supportive friend to decompress.

Crying or shaking does not make a man weak. It shows you are human. Telling your story with genuine emotion can actually bring deeper connection and empathy from listeners.

---

9. Inviting Others to Share Too

When a man opens up about his sadness or experiences with therapy, it can encourage other men to speak out as well. They might say, "I never told anyone this, but I felt the same way." This collective sharing can create a ripple effect, where each new voice gives more men permission to speak.

How to invite others:

- **Ask questions:** If you sense a friend is also struggling, ask them how they have been feeling.
- **Offer to listen:** Say, "If you ever need to talk, I'm here."
- **Show genuine curiosity:** If they start talking, pay full attention. Do not jump in with quick fixes or jokes.
- **Follow up:** Check in after a few days. This tells them you truly care, not just in the moment.

Being the first to open up requires courage, but the outcome can be powerful. Men often bond more deeply after sharing real feelings. It breaks the surface-level chat that leaves both sides feeling empty.

---

10. Knowing Your Boundaries

While sharing can help, no one is obligated to talk about every personal detail. It is vital to keep certain boundaries for your own emotional health. Some men might choose not to share specific traumatic events or family conflicts if they are not ready or the environment is not supportive.

Building healthy boundaries:

1. **Trust your gut:** If something feels too private or too raw, you have every right to keep it to yourself or wait until you feel safer.
2. **Use broad terms if needed:** Instead of describing the entire event, you can say, "I went through a hard situation a few years back." This acknowledges the struggle without giving details.
3. **Stop if it becomes distressing:** You can say, "I'm not comfortable going deeper right now." That is a complete sentence.
4. **Consider professional help:** If certain events cause severe emotional pain when mentioned, a therapist might be the best first place to explore them.

Men sometimes feel pressured to "bare it all" once they start talking. Remember that you are in control of your story. Deciding how much to share is your right.

---

11. The Relief of Being Heard

One of the main reasons sharing helps is that it ends the feeling that you are shouldering everything alone. When a man sees a listener nod with understanding or hear them say, "I get it, that sounds tough," it can release tension that built up for months or years.

Signs of a good listener:

- They focus on you, not their phone or other distractions.
- They do not judge or make light of your feelings.
- They ask questions that show genuine interest.
- They keep your information private if you asked them to.

Such experiences can shift your internal dialogue from "Nobody would understand" to "At least one person understands." That shift is huge in healing. It can lighten self-blame and support a sense of belonging.

---

12. Sharing with Family vs. Friends

Family members often play a role in how men see themselves, especially fathers or older male relatives. Telling them about your sadness can feel more intimidating than telling a coworker. The same is true for partners or spouses who might be directly impacted by your mood swings.

Points to consider for family sharing:

- **They might need time to adjust:** Some relatives are shocked to learn you have been struggling in silence. They might react by worrying or wanting to solve everything at once.
- **Explain what you need:** Perhaps you only want them to listen, not offer solutions right away.
- **Prepare for mixed responses:** Some family members might be super supportive, others might not know how to handle emotional talk. That does not invalidate your feelings.
- **Your partner might feel relief:** If you have been moody, your partner might have blamed themselves. Hearing your honest situation can clear misunderstandings.

Friends, on the other hand, might be easier to approach if you share common interests or known empathy. However, close friends can also be deeply affected by learning you are in pain. Being ready to answer questions or reassure them that you just need a caring ear can make the conversation smoother.

---

13. Sharing with Professionals

Sometimes sharing is best done with a counselor, psychologist, or psychiatrist. These professionals are trained to handle sensitive topics, and confidentiality rules mean your information stays private (unless there is a legal or immediate safety issue). Talking to a pro can bring relief because you do not have to worry about burdening them—this is their job, and they have the tools to help.

Why professional sharing might be key:

- **No bias or personal ties:** Unlike friends or family, a therapist does not have a personal stake in your choices. They can be neutral, focusing on your well-being.
- **Deeper insight:** Professionals can connect your stories to patterns of thinking or behavior you did not see.
- **Structured help:** They can offer worksheets, exercises, or a therapy plan that fits your experiences.

For men who fear being judged, the safe setting of a therapy office can be the first place they feel able to open up. Later, they might feel more prepared to share with loved ones in a balanced way.

14. When Sharing Feels Overwhelming

If you start talking about your story and become overwhelmed—crying hard, trembling, or feeling panic—it might mean you unearthed deeper trauma or strong emotions. Do not be alarmed. This is the body and mind's natural response to letting out bottled-up pain.

Ways to handle this safely:

- **Use grounding techniques:** Focus on your breathing. Name five things around you: something you can see, feel, smell, and so on, to stay connected to the present.
- **Ask for a short break:** If you are in a session, tell the listener you need a moment. Grab some water or step outside briefly.
- **Seek follow-up help:** If the feelings remain intense, contact a counselor. A single event of major emotional release might show that deeper healing is needed.
- **Avoid isolation:** After a strong reaction, do not immediately go off alone if you feel unstable. Ask a friend to stay with you or call someone to talk it through.

Overwhelm is not a sign you did something wrong. It simply means the emotions run deep. Moving slowly and getting professional help can turn those difficult moments into steps toward deeper relief.

15. Allowing Others to Share as Well

Sharing does not have to be a one-way flow. Encourage the people listening to talk about their thoughts too. This can balance the conversation and help you not feel like you are the only one with struggles. They might share stories about a time they felt low or a friend who overcame difficulties. This exchange of personal stories can create a network of empathy.

Tips for two-way sharing:

- **Show interest in their experiences:** Ask, "Has anything like this ever happened to you?"
- **Avoid turning it all on them:** Sometimes, we accidentally overshadow our own issue by focusing on the listener too much. Keep a balance.
- **Validate each other:** If they mention their own sadness, respond with understanding. Remind them that it is brave to talk about it.

This mutual conversation often builds trust quickly. It can shift a lonely sense of shame into a united feeling of, "We're both human, doing our best."

---

16. Recognizing Cultural or Community Factors

Different communities and cultures have their own traditions about talking openly. In some cultures, men are strongly discouraged from any sign of emotional vulnerability. In others, group sharing is common. Understanding the culture around you can guide how, when, and with whom you share.

Handling cultural challenges:

- **Respecting family views:** If your culture emphasizes keeping personal issues within the home, you might talk to a family elder. On the other hand, if your family is not supportive, an outside counselor might be safer.
- **Finding specialized groups:** Some support groups exist specifically for men of certain backgrounds, faiths, or life experiences. This can help you feel understood without explaining cultural context all the time.
- **Taking it slowly:** If your immediate circle strongly frowns upon talking about mental health, you can start in private settings or online groups where people are more open.

It is possible to respect your culture's values while also meeting your emotional needs. Sometimes that means carefully picking who you talk to, or educating relatives bit by bit about the reality of sadness and therapy.

---

17. The Ongoing Impact of Sharing

Once you open up, the story does not end. People might check on you later, asking how you are doing or offering continued support. This ongoing involvement can be a huge plus. However, it might also feel like pressure if you prefer to handle things on your own for a while.

Managing the aftermath:

- **Appreciate genuine concern:** If friends or family ask about your progress, they likely care about you. Thank them for their kindness.
- **Set personal limits:** If the questions become too frequent or uncomfortable, politely let them know you will reach out when you need help.
- **Review your own feelings:** Did sharing bring a sense of relief or an emotional drain? This can guide how you approach future sharing.

Talking about sadness is rarely a one-time event. It can evolve into deeper discussions, changing relationships, or even leading to new opportunities (like joining a support network or connecting with mentors who have faced similar issues).

---

18. Chapter Summary

Sharing your personal story of sadness or low mood can be a powerful move for mental health. It counters the belief that men must silently bear all burdens. Whether done privately with one trusted friend or publicly to raise awareness, talking about these issues can break isolation, invite support, and help other men recognize they are not alone in feeling overwhelmed.

Yet, sharing also requires care. A man should decide who to talk to, how much detail to provide, and whether the setting is safe. Preparation for possible negative feedback or intense emotional reactions is wise. By starting small and learning from each conversation, men can find the right balance between honesty and privacy.

Telling your story can feel scary, but it often leads to relief, deeper connections, and a broader sense of purpose. You may discover that speaking up not only improves your own journey toward better mental health but also encourages the men around you—family, friends, or coworkers—to seek help for their silent struggles. In the next chapter, we will turn to **Resources for Ongoing Support**, looking at local and online tools, financial assistance, and specialized services that men can use to keep building healthy minds and stable lives.

CHAPTER 19: RESOURCES FOR ONGOING SUPPORT

Men dealing with sadness often need help beyond what they can do on their own. Even if you have tried therapy, medication, or self-care habits, there may be times when you want fresh tools or a steady source of support. This chapter talks about practical resources that men can use in different life situations. It also points out some lesser-known or specialized services that might make a big difference. By knowing what is available, a man can pick the support that best fits his personal situation, whether it is local, online, or through a national group.

These resources can help you stay on track when faced with new stresses, family pressure, or a major life shift. They can also prevent a small setback from growing into a major crisis. Remember, asking for help shows responsibility, not weakness. By using these tools, you give yourself the best chance to live in a healthier way over the long term.

---

1. Local Community Centers and Groups

Many towns have community centers that hold events or run programs to help people in the neighborhood. Some of these might focus on men's health, general wellness, or mental health. You can drop by and ask if they have meetings or classes for people feeling sad or overwhelmed. Even if they do not have a specific men's group, they might point you to other local programs.

- **Advantages:** Local events let you meet people face-to-face. This can create personal connections that make it easier to stick to healthy habits.
- **Possible features:** Classes on stress management, casual sports leagues, or small discussion circles.
- **Finding them:** Check your city or county website. Libraries or local government buildings often post flyers for these centers.

A man might think these places are only for children's programs or older folks. But often, they have wide-ranging activities. If you do not find what you need, politely suggest it. Sometimes, centers are open to adding new sessions if they see real interest.

2. Support Lines and Hotlines

Talking on the phone can be a fast way to get relief if you feel panic rising or if you have no one nearby to confide in. Many regions have free hotlines staffed by trained listeners who understand crisis situations. They can also direct you to local services like counseling or safe housing if needed.

- **Examples of calls you can make:**
    - National suicide prevention hotlines (for emergency emotional support)
    - Lines specializing in men's mental health or fatherhood stress
    - General mental health support numbers that offer crisis counseling

These hotlines often run 24/7, so you are never stuck waiting for business hours. Men sometimes avoid calling because they do not see themselves as being in a dire situation. But hotlines are not only for extreme crises. You can call if you need to talk, if you feel unsafe in your thoughts, or if you just want direction about next steps.

---

3. Employee Assistance Programs (EAPs)

If you have a job, check whether your company offers an Employee Assistance Program. EAPs usually provide short-term counseling or referrals for longer therapy at no or low cost. They can also help with practical matters like legal advice or financial counseling, which might lower stress that feeds sadness.

- **How they work:** You call a special number, speak to a counselor, and they connect you with local services. Some programs include in-person sessions, while others are phone-based.
- **Privacy:** These programs keep your information confidential. Most employers do not see the details of who uses the EAP or why.
- **Advantages:** Fast access, little to no cost, and it does not require searching for a private therapist on your own.

EAPs are an underrated resource because many workers forget they exist or assume they are only for big problems. In reality, if your mental health is slipping, an EAP might prevent a deeper slump. Plus, it shows your employer that you are proactively caring for yourself, which can help you remain steady on the job.

4. Online Therapy Platforms

Virtual therapy has become more common. Through video calls, voice calls, or even text-based sessions, you can talk to a licensed professional without leaving home. This is useful for men in rural areas, those with tight schedules, or people who feel uneasy waiting in a therapist's office.

- **How to choose a platform:** Look for ones that list the credentials of their therapists. Check if they allow you to switch therapists if you do not find a good fit right away. Read reviews from other users.
- **Privacy:** Most reputable platforms use secure connections. You can talk from your home or even from your car if privacy is an issue.
- **Insurance coverage:** Some insurance plans now cover online therapy. You can also check the platform's prices or sliding-scale fees if you have a lower income.

For men who travel a lot for work or have unpredictable schedules, online therapy means less worry about missing sessions. You can chat from a hotel room or during a break. The main caution is to ensure the platform is legitimate and the therapist is licensed in your state or region.

---

5. Specialized Men's Health Clinics

Some clinics focus specifically on men's health, including mental health. These might include checks of hormone levels, stress tests, and counseling tailored to male problems like aggression, shame about sadness, or fatherhood pressures. If you suspect that low testosterone is adding to your sad mood, or you want a place that understands male social roles, these clinics might help.

- **Services they might offer:**
    - Testing hormone levels and offering safe treatments if needed.
    - Counseling for men who feel they cannot talk to a "regular" therapist.
    - Guidance on diet and exercise that fits male biology.

While not every city has a dedicated men's health center, some general clinics have men-focused branches. Look up "Men's Health Clinic" or "Men's Wellness Center" in your area. This option might cost more, depending on insurance coverage, but it can save time by combining physical and emotional care under one roof.

6. Veteran Support Services

Men who served in the military often face unique forms of sadness or stress, including post-traumatic stress. Many countries have veteran support groups, health clinics, and even phone lines specifically for those who served. These places understand the culture of the military, the challenges of returning to civilian life, and the internal scars that remain after service.

- **Possible resources:**
    - Veteran Affairs (VA) hospitals or clinics for mental health check-ups
    - Veteran peer support groups, sometimes run by nonprofit groups
    - Financial and job placement help for vets who are struggling to reintegrate

If you are a veteran, ignoring these services can mean missing out on specialized care. Having peers who share a similar background can reduce shame and help you open up. Even if your time in the service was many years ago, these resources can still apply to you.

---

7. Faith-Based Support

Some men find comfort in faith-based programs or counseling. Many churches, synagogues, or mosques have staff or volunteers who provide pastoral counseling. They might not be licensed therapists (though some are), but they can offer an understanding ear and spiritual guidance. If you are religious, this connection can bring hope and a sense of larger meaning during low times.

- **Examples:**
    - One-on-one sessions with a pastor or spiritual leader
    - Faith-based small groups that discuss personal struggles and how faith can help
    - Retreats or workshops focused on healing and mental well-being

Make sure that the leader or counselor is open to professional mental health approaches if needed. If someone says, "Just pray and you'll be fine," that might not match your real needs. However, a balanced faith-based program can offer both spiritual insight and practical coping tools.

8. Groups for Men with Specific Challenges

Aside from general support groups, there are also groups aimed at particular problems or life stages. These can include men going through divorce, single fathers, men with chronic illness, or survivors of abuse. Being around others who truly "get it" can speed up the sense of belonging and trust.

- **Benefits:**
    - Shared experiences reduce the need to explain everything from scratch.
    - Group members might have "golden gem" tips that most others do not know, like legal shortcuts or ways to handle certain triggers.
    - You can see examples of men who overcame a similar challenge, which can bring hope.

To find such groups, search online or ask local mental health professionals. Libraries or community centers might also let certain specialty groups use their meeting rooms. Even if you cannot attend weekly, occasional visits can remind you that your concerns are not unique.

---

9. Financial Aid for Treatment

Cost is a huge barrier for many men, especially if they have no insurance or their coverage is limited. But giving up on professional help due to money might lead to bigger costs later, like missed work or medical bills if your mental health gets worse. Several financial supports exist:

- **Sliding-scale therapists:** Some private counselors adjust fees based on a person's income. You can ask about this upfront.
- **Nonprofit clinics:** Local mental health nonprofits sometimes have free or lower-priced counseling. They might have waitlists, so sign up early.
- **Grants or charitable funds:** A few organizations sponsor therapy sessions if you meet certain conditions, like being a low-income father or a young adult at risk.
- **Online mental health funds:** Crowdfunding or charitable sites occasionally help people pay for therapy or medication. This takes planning, but it is an option if you are truly out of funds.

Never assume you cannot afford help without exploring these possibilities. Even a few sessions can offer a path out of a slump. Pride sometimes stops men from seeking financial help, but remember that mental health is as vital as physical health.

10. Workplace Benefits Beyond EAPs

Aside from Employee Assistance Programs, some workplaces offer mental health days or flexible schedules so employees can attend therapy. Others have onsite gyms or mindfulness classes. If you are not sure, ask your Human Resources department about well-being benefits. They might not promote them much, but they exist.

- **Possible extras:**
    - Paid or unpaid leave for mental health recovery
    - Subsidies for gym memberships or wellness apps
    - Company-run workshops on reducing stress or building positive habits

Using these perks does not mean you are weak. It signals that you value your health enough to use all the tools at your disposal. In fact, employers often prefer workers who look after their health rather than those who hide problems until they become big crises.

11. Coaching and Mentoring

A life coach or mentor is not always a mental health professional, but they can assist with specific goals that overlap with emotional well-being. For instance, a coach might help you improve your time management or learn new coping strategies for daily stress. Mentors, often older or more experienced men, can give guidance based on life wisdom.

- **Difference from therapy:** A therapist delves into deeper emotional issues and uses specific treatment techniques. A coach or mentor might focus more on forward-looking tasks or career goals.
- **Selecting a coach:** Look for someone with credible training. Check reviews or speak to past clients. Some are better suited to men's issues than others.

- **Mentoring programs:** These could be volunteer-based, such as local business associations or fatherhood programs, where experienced men help younger men navigate challenges.

While a coach cannot replace therapy for serious sadness, they can add structure to your life. This might keep you engaged and enthusiastic, lowering the risk of slipping back into negative thought patterns.

---

12. Free Educational Resources

The internet has a wealth of free tools for men seeking better mental health. These include articles, videos, and even online courses. The key is to pick reputable sources, because not all advice on the web is reliable. Government health websites, well-known clinics, and universities often post solid information.

- **Possible freebies:**
    - Worksheets on managing negative thoughts
    - Lists of local support groups, updated regularly
    - Webinars by psychologists on stress relief or anger management
    - Guided meditations or relaxation audio files

If reading is not your thing, look for short videos or audio podcasts you can hear during your commute. Keeping these resources at hand can remind you that help is never far away. They also serve as a starting point if you are nervous about reaching out to a professional.

---

13. Helplines or Apps for Specific Issues (Less Known)

Some men face less common problems like gambling addiction, hoarding, or very specialized anxieties. Thanks to technology, there are now helplines or apps for these narrow concerns. For instance:

- **Quitlines for smoking** or vaping, where you can get a coach.
- **Gambling hotlines** that connect you with local addiction counselors.
- **Digital habit trackers** for OCD-like behaviors, offering daily tips and reminders.

- **Post-hospital transition lines** that help men re-adjust after a hospital stay.

These specialized tools can be golden for men who felt no general hotline understood their specific problem. By focusing on a tight niche, these services often gather more precise knowledge and can connect you to specialized therapy or local experts.

14. College or University Services

If you are a student, universities usually have counseling centers offering free or cheap sessions. Even if you are not enrolled, some university psychology departments provide low-cost therapy overseen by licensed psychologists. The sessions might be led by graduate students in training, but they follow strict supervision rules to ensure quality.

- **Advantages:**
    - Lower fees than private therapy
    - Flexible hours that fit student or working adult schedules
    - Possible exposure to newer treatment methods or research-based care

If you worry about seeing a counselor in training, remember they are typically monitored by experienced professors. This can actually lead to more thorough care, as your case might receive additional attention and discussion in the department. Check local colleges' websites for their psychology clinic or counseling center.

15. Men's Sheds and Community Workshops

In some parts of the world, "Men's Sheds" or workshop-style gatherings bring men together to do hands-on projects like woodworking or repairing old items. These activities give men a space to talk casually while working, which can feel more comfortable than sitting in a circle and talking face-to-face. The main aim is social connection and skill sharing, but it often reduces feelings of isolation.

- **Typical features:**

- An actual workshop space with tools
            - Regular meetups where men fix or build items together
            - Informal chats that let people open up about life
    - **Finding them:**
        - Look for "Men's Shed" or "Men's Workshop" groups in your region.
        - Sometimes charities sponsor these spaces for retired men or anyone who wants to learn.

Men who do not like formal groups might prefer the practical focus of a Men's Shed. It offers companionship without pressure to talk about emotions openly, though emotional support often emerges naturally over time.

---

16. Long-Term Rehabilitation Centers

If sadness has led to severe substance use or other major life disruptions, a long-term rehab center might be an option. These are not only for alcohol or drug problems; some centers also address deep emotional trauma or co-occurring mental health problems. The stay can last weeks or months, giving a structured environment to learn coping methods.

- **What they provide:**
    - Therapy sessions (group and individual)
    - Classes on life skills, anger control, or stress management
    - A safe space away from triggers
- **Paying for it:**
    - Some insurance plans cover part of the cost
    - Nonprofit-run centers may have scholarships
    - Sliding-scale fees or payment plans might be offered

Going to a rehab center is a serious step, but for men caught in destructive cycles, it can be a game-changer. Living onsite with a routine takes you out of chaotic environments and allows full focus on healing.

---

17. Checking for Up-To-Date Resource Lists

Organizations sometimes lose funding, move locations, or change phone numbers, so an old resource list might be out of date. Always confirm details before relying on a single flyer or website from years ago. You can do this by calling or emailing the place in question. Libraries, health departments, and major nonprofits often keep current directories of mental health services. Taking the time to verify can save you from frustration later.

This is also true when you share resource info with friends. Give them the newest details you have, or point them to a directory that is updated regularly. If they face an emergency, outdated info can cause delays that make things worse.

---

18. Chapter Summary

Long-lasting support can come from many sources. You do not have to rely solely on your own willpower or a single therapist. By exploring local community centers, specialized hotlines, faith-based groups, or even men-focused clinics, you expand your safety net. Online therapy, employee programs, and no- or low-cost counseling are also out there to fit different budgets and lifestyles.

This chapter touched on many types of help, including niche services for veterans, men with specific problems, or those who prefer certain environments like men's workshops. The main point is that if you feel stuck, it is worth looking around for a resource that matches your current need. That might mean a phone call to a crisis line, signing up for an EAP session, or joining a local group for divorced fathers. Each step can make it easier to maintain mental health gains and avoid sinking into deeper sadness.

Next, **CHAPTER 20** will focus on **Planning for a Better Future**. We will cover ways to look ahead with a clear head, such as creating a personal "wellness blueprint," managing fears of relapse, and balancing responsibilities so you can keep growing. By combining the resources in this chapter with a forward-looking plan, men can walk a steadier path toward feeling well and living with more purpose.

CHAPTER 20: PLANNING FOR A BETTER FUTURE

When men have worked hard to handle their sadness—using therapy, self-help, family support, or specialized resources—they often wonder what comes next. Is the process ever truly finished? How can someone keep from sliding backward? This final chapter focuses on creating a personal roadmap for ongoing well-being. It is about looking ahead with hope while staying realistic about the need for continued attention to mental health.

We will talk about forming a personal "wellness blueprint," staying aware of red flags, and making sure the progress achieved so far does not fade in the face of new stresses. We will also address how to handle big life events that might challenge your stability—like switching jobs, moving, or dealing with loss in the family. By the end, you should have concrete ideas on how to maintain the healthier self you have worked so hard to build.

---

1. Recognizing Growth and Setting Fresh Targets

A good first step is to look back at what you have already overcome. Men sometimes focus only on their flaws and forget the gains made. If you used to feel hopeless every day but now manage your mood most of the time, that is real progress. If you once avoided talking to anyone about your sadness and now have at least one supportive friend or therapist, you have grown.

How to measure your growth:

1. **Compare old daily habits to new ones:** Are you eating better or sleeping more regularly than before?
2. **Reflect on emotional changes:** Do you bounce back from stress faster or handle conflict with less anger?
3. **Note big achievements:** Such as finishing a course of therapy, ending harmful habits, or repairing a strained relationship.

After acknowledging these steps forward, think about the next goals. They do not have to be huge. Maybe you want to keep a stable routine or begin a small side project that excites you. These fresh targets keep you moving, so you do not settle into stagnation.

---

2. Building a Personalized Wellness Blueprint

This blueprint is like a manual you design for yourself, showing what keeps you balanced and what might trigger a downturn. It can be a document on your computer or a notebook you keep handy. When life gets chaotic, this plan reminds you of your core supports and your best coping methods.

- **Sections to include:**
    1. **Daily practices:** The small habits that lift or protect your mood (e.g., 15-minute walk, checking in with a friend, short breathing drill).
    2. **Red flags:** Specific signs that you might be sliding (e.g., skipping meals, withdrawing from loved ones).
    3. **Action steps for red flags:** Who to call, what to read, or which tactic to use if these signs appear.
    4. **Long-term goals:** Milestones you hope to reach in six months or a year, plus the steps to get there.
    5. **Resources list:** Phone numbers of your doctor, counselor, hotlines, or supportive friends.

Review this blueprint every so often. If your situation changes—say you move cities or end a relationship—you can update it. The goal is to have a go-to reference when stress hits, so you do not waste energy trying to remember what worked in the past.

---

3. Keeping Self-Awareness High

Being aware of your own emotional state is a powerful defense against sliding back into deep sadness. It means noticing not just the big crises but also the everyday signals of rising stress. This self-awareness can include both emotional and physical cues.

- **Examples of emotional cues:** Irritability, impatience, or a sense of dread about the day.
- **Examples of physical cues:** Headaches, constant tiredness, or stomachaches.

Men often push through physical discomfort without linking it to mental strain. By pausing to notice patterns—like tension in your shoulders on work nights—you can step in early with coping actions. This might be a short walk, a breathing exercise, or a talk with someone supportive. Over time, this habit of checking in with yourself becomes second nature.

---

4. Maintaining Relationships That Support You

A better future often depends on not going it alone. The friendships or family ties you have nurtured during your improvement are still key. Make time to see or call the people who helped you, even if you feel you are doing better now. Staying connected keeps you from drifting into isolation, which can trigger negative thought patterns.

- **Ways to keep relationships strong:**
    - Schedule a monthly catch-up with a friend, either in person or by phone.
    - Remember special dates like birthdays or milestones and send a note.
    - Offer help in return. If someone was there for you, you can show up for them too.

If you used a men's group, a therapy circle, or an online forum, consider staying active there, even if you do not attend as often. Regular contact keeps your social safety net in place. It also reminds you that giving support can be as uplifting as receiving it.

---

5. Handling Major Life Changes

Life events like moving, changing jobs, getting married, or going through a breakup can shake your routines. Even good changes add stress. Recognizing that these shifts might destabilize your mental state helps you prepare.

- **Preventive actions:**
    - **Plan therapy check-ins:** If you know a big change is coming (like a new baby or a move), schedule an extra session with your counselor or mentor.
    - **Delegate tasks:** Ask friends or family for help with packing, childcare, or other duties so you are not overloaded.

- **Review your blueprint:** Update it to reflect the new environment or responsibilities. Maybe your old workout routine will not fit your new schedule, so plan a fresh one.

Accept that it is normal to feel uncertain or emotional during transitions. Sticking to core habits (like decent sleep and simple mindfulness) can keep you grounded until the new situation settles in.

---

6. Expecting and Handling Small Setbacks

Just because you have improved does not mean you will never have a low day or a difficult week. Sadness or old triggers might return in smaller doses. The difference now is that you have tools and experiences to manage them better.

- **Use your setback plan:** Recall Chapter 16's strategies—notice early signs, ask for help, and adjust routines if needed.
- **Avoid panic thinking:** A slump does not mean you are back at square one. Remind yourself of past successes.
- **Stay flexible:** If you see a pattern of repeated stress, maybe a new approach is needed. Talk to a professional if you feel stuck.

Men who continue to do well often treat setbacks as normal speed bumps. They adjust quickly instead of letting guilt or fear keep them from acting.

---

7. Exploring New Interests

Sometimes men discover that after dealing with sadness, they have extra energy and a desire to try things they once put off. This can be starting a small side business, learning an instrument, or taking up a creative hobby. These pursuits can add a sense of meaning beyond just "not feeling sad."

- **Why new interests help:**
    - They bring fresh social connections, especially if you join a class or club.
    - They foster self-esteem as you gain new skills.
    - They fill your free time with purposeful activity rather than letting negative thoughts creep back.

Pick something that feels exciting or meaningful, not just another "should." If you have always wanted to learn a language or help out at a local shelter, now might be the right time. These new interests can keep your outlook bright and maintain momentum.

8. Balancing Self-Care with Responsibilities

Men sometimes swing from ignoring their own needs to spending all day on self-help tasks. The better path is a balance: keep up your health routines while handling work and family duties. If you spend too much time focusing on mental health, you might neglect finances or relationships. If you only focus on work, stress might return quickly.

Tips for balance:

- **Schedule self-care:** Block out certain times for exercise or rest. This ensures you do not forget yourself when life gets busy.
- **Use shorter but consistent sessions:** Ten minutes of mindfulness daily might be more useful than an hour once a month.
- **Involve family or friends:** Invite them to join you in a quick walk or a healthy meal. This merges your well-being with time spent together.

Balance does not mean each part of life is always perfect. It means you do not allow one area to drain all your energy. Pay attention to small signals of imbalance, such as feeling cranky or noticing tasks piling up at home. Then adjust as needed.

9. Guarding Against Overconfidence

After men see a big improvement, they might think they are done with all forms of sadness. This can lead to dropping healthy habits because they believe they are "fixed." Overconfidence can be risky. Old negative thoughts or behaviors can creep back if you stop checking in with yourself.

- **Stay humble:** Recognize that mental health is an ongoing process, not a final trophy.
- **Keep essential routines:** Do not abandon all exercise, therapy check-ins, or journaling just because you feel better. Reduce them if needed, but avoid stopping abruptly.

- **Continue learning:** Read new articles, watch videos on advanced coping techniques, or talk to mentors. A broad knowledge base can protect you from future pitfalls.

Think of it like physical fitness: just because you got in shape once does not mean you can stop all workouts forever. Maintaining mental health also needs a steady approach, even if it is at a lower intensity.

---

10. Considering Giving Back

Men who have made solid improvements sometimes feel drawn to help others who are still struggling. This could be mentoring a younger man, volunteering with a mental health group, or simply offering a supportive ear to friends. Sharing the lessons you learned might even strengthen your own progress, as teaching often reinforces what you know.

- **Ways to give back:**
    - **Peer support:** Join a program where you counsel men who face sadness or anxiety.
    - **Public speaking:** If you are comfortable, talk briefly at community centers or youth groups about coping with low mood.
    - **Online Q&A:** Answer questions in forums from people who are just starting therapy or worried about medication.
    - **Organizing social events:** Plan small gatherings for men who want to bond or do productive activities together.

Helping others should not be a burden. Do it within your limits. If you start feeling overwhelmed, step back and take care of yourself first. But if done wisely, giving back can fill your life with added purpose and keep you connected to helpful communities.

---

11. Having a Crisis Backup Plan

Even the best mental health routine can face a crisis due to tragedy, severe financial stress, or a health scare. When major events strike, men might freeze. This is where a crisis backup plan is vital. Think of it as a safety net if everything starts feeling overwhelming.

- **What to include:**
  - **Emergency contact person:** A close friend or family member you can call day or night.
  - **Medical info:** If you have medication or a history of certain treatments, list them so people can help you if you are in bad shape.
  - **Crisis line numbers:** Keep them in your phone or wallet.
  - **Short instructions:** If you get into a mental fog, you might need to see a quick list of steps: call your therapist, do a breathing drill, contact your emergency contact.

Men often skip forming a crisis plan, believing it is negative thinking. But it is actually being practical and prepared. Having that plan can be comforting, letting you know that if a severe storm hits, you have a route to safer ground.

---

12. Using Technology Wisely

Apps and digital trackers can help keep mental health in good shape. For instance, there are mood-tracking apps that let you log how you feel daily, plus note triggers or big events. Over time, patterns emerge. Some apps provide guided meditations, daily tasks, or quick notes of encouragement. Even reminders for therapy sessions or medication can reduce slip-ups.

- **Choosing the right tools:**
  - **Check privacy:** Make sure the app does not share your data without your consent.
  - **Look for credible sources:** Apps tied to recognized health organizations or well-known mental health experts may be more reliable.
  - **Avoid overload:** Too many apps can become stressful. Pick one or two that truly help.

A man who travels or has a chaotic schedule might find these digital aids especially handy. Just keep an eye on screen time; if using apps becomes a source of stress, simplify your approach.

---

13. Keeping Positive Influences in Media

What you watch, read, or listen to each day can affect your mood more than you realize. Constant news about disasters or following social media accounts that make you feel inadequate can drag you down. While you cannot shut out the entire world, you can choose to include positive or balanced media sources.

- **Practical ideas:**
    - Follow uplifting pages that focus on real solutions to problems.
    - Limit how often you check the news, maybe once or twice a day, instead of having it on constantly.
    - Subscribe to podcasts or channels that teach productive habits rather than only dwelling on negative topics.

This does not mean pretending everything is fine in the world. It means not drowning yourself in bleak or aggressive content every spare minute. Find a healthy media balance that keeps you informed but not overwhelmed.

---

14. Checking in with a Professional Sometimes

Even if your sadness seems in the past, a professional check-up every few months or once a year can catch any slow return of negative patterns. Think of it like going to the doctor for a regular physical. A short mental health check might reveal early warning signs or provide a tune-up for your coping skills.

- **Possible forms of check-ups:**
    - A single session with your former therapist to see how you are doing.
    - An online questionnaire that measures your current anxiety or depression levels.
    - A chat with a trusted mentor who can give honest feedback on whether you seem more stressed than usual.

These check-ins can help you adapt your wellness blueprint if your life circumstances change. It is always easier to handle small mood drops than to wait for a full-blown relapse.

15. Exploring Next-Level Self-Development

Feeling stable does not have to be the end goal. Some men decide to aim higher, exploring deeper personal growth. That could be building emotional intelligence to connect better with loved ones or developing leadership qualities to succeed in a new job role.

- **Options for deeper growth:**
    - **Workshops on emotional intelligence:** These teach ways to recognize and handle not only your emotions but also those of others.
    - **Programs on resilience:** Some groups focus on how to bounce back quickly from all sorts of life pressures, using proven strategies.
    - **Mindful living courses:** Going beyond basic breathing drills to a fuller approach that includes mindful eating, mindful conversations, etc.

These advanced pursuits can replace the emptiness that sometimes appears when men no longer struggle daily. Instead of drifting, you can direct your mental energy toward improving quality of life and relationships even further.

---

16. Teaching Healthy Patterns to Younger Men

If you have children, nephews, or younger cousins, you can pass on healthy habits so they do not repeat the same mistakes. Show them it is okay to talk about emotions, seek help, and not be perfect. You might encourage them to do short reflections or talk about their feelings in a calm setting. The impact can be huge, shaping a new generation of men who see mental health care as normal.

- **Ways to teach gently:**
    - Encourage open discussions about daily highs and lows at meal times.
    - Model apologies and honesty if you lose your temper, so they see it is possible to own up and move on.
    - Share simple coping skills, like how to do a quick breathing exercise or a walk when feeling upset.

By guiding younger men, you also keep your own lessons fresh. Teaching often cements what you have learned. It becomes a continuous reminder of what healthy living looks like for your mind.

17. Staying Aware of Social Shifts

The conversation around men's mental health is changing, with more public figures openly discussing their emotional struggles. Keep an eye on these shifts. They might bring new local groups or updated laws that cover mental health as part of insurance. Being aware can open extra doors for you or someone you know.

- **Where to see these trends:**
    - Articles about men's issues in reputable magazines or websites
    - Campaigns by sports figures or actors talking about sadness
    - Workplace changes that add more mental health days or staff training

If you spot something useful—like a new men's mental health meet-up—consider checking it out. Social progress can widen your network of helpers or give you fresh angles on problems. You might also find ways to advocate for even better policies at your job or in your neighborhood.

---

18. Chapter Summary

Planning for a better future is about more than just avoiding sadness. It involves sustaining what you have built, staying prepared for life's twists, and continuing to grow in new directions. A personal wellness blueprint keeps your daily habits, warning signs, and key resources in one place. Regular self-awareness helps catch the first hint of trouble so that you can respond calmly.

Maintaining supportive relationships, balancing responsibilities, and guarding against overconfidence all safeguard your mental well-being in the long term. Though setbacks may still arise, you now have the experience and tools to handle them. You can even go further: exploring new hobbies, improving emotional intelligence, or mentoring younger men who might face the same old messages about "toughness."

You do not have to be perfect. A better future is about steady improvement, with ups and downs along the way. But by using the wisdom from earlier chapters—plus the ongoing support of friends, family, professionals, or community groups—you can keep moving toward a life that feels more stable, more fulfilled, and more in line with the person you want to be.

Conclusion of the Book

We have covered many aspects of sadness and mental health in men, from warning signs and causes to treatments, daily habits, and long-term planning. The key points to remember are:

1. Sadness does not define you. It is a health issue that you can address.
2. There is no shame in reaching out—friends, family, counselors, and online resources all play roles in healing.
3. Harmful habits can be changed if you spot and replace them with better daily routines.
4. It is wise to combine methods: therapy, self-care, medication if needed, and staying connected with supportive people.
5. Setbacks are normal. They do not cancel your progress. Act early, use your coping tools, and ask for help when the load is too heavy.

Above all, keep hope. Men in many cultures have broken free from the idea that they must never talk about sadness. By reading and applying these chapters, you have already taken steps that many do not. Keep building on that. Follow your personal wellness plan, remain open to learning, and remember you are not alone—there are always sources of support out there, ready for you. Take them, use them, and keep moving forward toward a healthier, more balanced life.